Cheltenham
B E T R A Y E D

Cheltenham
B E T R A Y E D

BY TIMOTHY MOWL

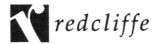

redcliffe

First published in 1995 by Redcliffe Press

ISBN 1 87297 114 8

British Library Cataloguing-in-Publication Data
CIP data for this book is available from the British Library

REDCLIFFE PRESS
Halsgrove House
Lower Moor Way
Tiverton EX16 6SS

Telephone: 01884 243242
Facsimile: 01884 243325

Printed in Great Britain by Longdunn Press Ltd, Bristol.

Contents

To my Mother.

The Author

Timothy Mowl gained an MA in Fine Arts and Literature from Birmingham University in 1978 and his doctorate in Architectural History from Oxford University in 1981. Since then he has become one of the country's leading architectural historians, lecturing both in England and North America. His many publications include *Trumpet at a Distant Gate – the Lodge as Prelude to the County House* (1985); a biography of the architect of Georgian Bath, *John Wood, Architect of Obsession* (1988); an indictment of twentieth century planning in Bath, entitled *The Sack of Bath and After* (1989); *To Build a Second City – Architects and Craftsmen of Georgian Bristol* (1991) and *Elizabethan and Jacobean Style* (1993). He has just completed a major study of the architecture of Cromwell's England entitled, *Architecture Without Kings*, which will be published by Manchester University Press in July 1995 His next book will be a biography of the mid-eighteenth century dilettante and Gothick fancier, Horace Walpole, to be published in 1997.

Timothy Mowl is a fellow of The Society of Antiquaries and was, for ten years, the South West regional representative of the Georgian Group, responsible for comment on conservation matters in the area. He is Chairman of Architecture and Design in the West of England and President of the Cheltenham Civic Society. Having worked for English Heritage as an Inspector of Historic Buildings, he is now a freelance writer and consultant on architecture and planning matters, most recently writing in Bath as the *Evening Chronicle's* architectural correspondent. At Bristol University where he lectures in the History of Art Department, he goes under the evocative title of the Giovanni Niccolo Servandoni Trust Fellow in Architectural History.

Acknowledgements

I should like to thank the Summerfield Trust for making this project financially possible with a generous grant, particularly Mrs Lavinia Sidgwick for her patient response to my occasional crises. Cheltenham is fortunate in such an institution and I am grateful, though he never had much time for me when I was in his shop, to the late Ronald Summerfield. If everyone left their fortunes as wisely as he did the world would be a better place.

Then my very warm thanks to all my friends in the Civic Society who have given me such solid backing and such practical support when I needed information, opinions, documentation or legal advice. In particular I wish to name Harry Benson whose idea it was that I should write this book; John Barnicoat, a former Secretary of the Society, who has answered all my queries with great efficiency and infectious enthusiasm, and Ken Pollock, whose lines of approach and solutions to the town's problems have underpinned much of my writing – this book is in many ways one that, given the time, Ken could have written himself. My thanks also to Kenneth Detheridge, Steve Stokes and Elizabeth Chaffers.

As usual my friend and co-author on other books, Brian Earnshaw, has been a constant source of helpful research and advice; Gordon Kelsey has worked wonders with my photography; Sir Colin Stansfield Smith was generous with his views on inner city regeneration; Councillor Robert Wilson answered my many queries about the Cheltenham political scene; Steven Blake directed me to photographs of lost buildings; Nigel Temple was informative about Abbeyholme; Anna Eavis and Moira Birks at the National Monuments Record were particularly sensitive to my pressing telephone calls; Huw Jones and Gerhard Hattingh supplied information and illustrative material on the Percy Thomas Partnership's two buildings for The Park campus; Barrie Pierce of Guilor Petch Architects sent material on their current projects, John Thatcher of the Falconer Partnership was helpful over the Royscot House site, and Mark Ashford of Beaufort Homes allowed illustration of the new terrace on Montpellier Spa Road. Last, but not least, I must thank my wife, Sarah, who has listened patiently to all my arguments and endured my passion for a town for which she feels little warmth.

If you are one of the great mass of Cheltenham people reading this book and feel just the least bit guilty about your previous indifference to your home, one of the most beautiful towns of Europe, please make amends by joining and strengthening the Civic Society now and becoming an active participant in every debate that concerns the town's welfare and its unique architectural charm. If we are not alert we will move into a Euro-era where decisions shift from democracy to bureaucracy. Experts are no more to be relied upon than you or me. On our home ground we are all experts.

Timothy Mowl
Bristol, Spring 1995

Introduction

This book has been written because I owe Cheltenham a personal debt of gratitude and because I believe the town needs defenders. This was where I was educated and where for a time I worked. In that first autumn when I arrived here Mods and Rockers were battling it out in the Promenade; the waters of Sandford's Art Deco Lido were unheated, icy cold but thronged with bathers; conkers showered down from that grove of chestnut trees that is only a memory now but which then still gave an unexpected dark magic to an otherwise sunlit shopping centre. Over the whole town Regency house fronts were in delicate decay; most, however, still survived. There was The Priory in melancholy pomp on London Road, Abbeyholme before its fall, and from my flat on Bayshill with its Vitruvian balcony there was a view of villas down the other side of the road, all intact and with trees in every garden.

It was a great town in which to grow up, a great town in which to become architecturally aware of both stylistic excess and minimalist classical refinement. And there was so much of it, so many streets, parks and suburbs to enjoy that you could never imagine the place would ever be seriously threatened by developers. They were, in any case, busy at that time ravaging more profitable towns like Wolverhampton and Birmingham in the

A mouldering terrace on St George's Place with Dr Jenner's house.

name of progress, full employment and personal profit. Cheltenham fell very late, after Bristol, Bath and Exeter. It was only when I came back to the town, by now the new President of the Civic Society, that I understood something that had initially puzzled me – why I had ever been elected to that honorary seeming office. I had first-hand experience of the Sack of Bath and had played a small part in the defence of that still beleaguered city. Now here was Cheltenham in a similar case, in need of the same defence, not so much sacked as seduced, case by case, villa by villa, its councillors full of good intentions, its developers eager to cash in on an existing urban beauty while offering nothing in exchange but banal buildings, wrecked gardens and overcrowded roads.

What was so striking to me, coming from one spa town to another, was the difference in civic attitudes, Cheltenham's bewildering lack of self-confidence. Bath was alert and proud, alive with anger at the despoilers. Cheltenham, with the honourable exception of the small Civic Society and a few stalwarts, was indifferent to the pillage, even a little flattered by it, as if a bad new building was a mark of favour from on high, an unexpected attention to a weary old courtesan who had come to expect her lovers to look elsewhere. The local paper, that might reasonably be expected to aim high in a middle class town, famous for its standards of education and hoping to host a university, was a down-market tabloid that served business and commercial advertisers first and was on most issues a mere replica of its national parent, the *Daily Mail*.

Most disturbingly, and this is what has made me write with a sense of urgency, that national tendency to despair of democratic solutions, and to turn to experts from Brussels for direction, had its local equivalent. The Liberal Democrat majority on the Borough Council, in contradiction of the party's name, was using an initiative by the Chief Executive (only a grander title for the old style Town Clerk) for a quick fix solution of massive development to the unemployment problem. Unemployment is in no way peculiar to Cheltenham. It is a national phenomenon that we all have to live with in an age of mechanisation and computers. No one expects Reg Ward's 'Bid' – 'Cheltenham Millennium' – to be imposed in all its grandiose ruthlessness, but in such projects it is customary to demand 200% sacrifices and then leave the victim relieved and grateful when only 100% ruin has been inflicted.

Cheltenham cannot afford that 100% destruction. Having personally suffered and enjoyed that vulnerability to change, that flexibility of employment which most of us experience these days, I am not blind to the problems of being out of work. What I suggest here is that Cheltenham should not allow the emotional pressures of that problem to rush its Council into potentially destructive and ineffective grand solutions for the new Millennium. More roads, more shops and more office premises, for a town already plagued with too much traffic and littered with boarded-up shops and un-let offices, is a step into the dark. It would be one of those bold enterprises that towns spend the next twenty years paying for in their council taxes and regretting for its visual vandalism. Anyone in any doubt as to the realities of the projected development should walk the St James's site and take in those two dreary hulks of uninspired building that already occupy it.

Cheltenham's face is her only real fortune. It is not a place in which to make quick profits or macho political reputations, but one of Britain's rare urban spaces of generous and achieved quality. We owe it our awareness and our vigilance.

Lansdown Station in its Grecian prime, a wonderfully atmospheric gateway to a classical spa town (Rokeby Collection).

Lansdown Station today, seen from the same angle. Even the cars are uglier and one pathetic Doric half column survives from the splendid former propylaeum.

A Town of Thin Loyalties

Writing on Cheltenham in the very early 1950s, John Betjeman still saw it as a town 'preserved almost entirely by the military', a place of lace curtains and bootmakers, of shops for ladies whose high coiled hair required extra large hats. While lyrically aware of a town where the lonely widows of colonels and major generals sat knitting in the lounges of retirement hotels, Betjeman had a strong sense of how little time there

The new face of Cheltenham.

was before the military generations would die out and the town's frail and complex beauty would be left without its traditional guardians. 'The aesthetes must help them,' he wrote and he hoped that a recently formed Cheltenham Regency Society would save a lovely town from 'careerist civil servants and greedy speculators'.

Now, forty-five years later, it has to be said that the aesthetes did not come to help the old military men and that the 'careerists and greedy speculators' have had a field day with the town.

The interesting question is how a place of such distinction ever came to depend upon a thin strata of alien retirees for its character and for its aesthetic watchmen. There is, in fact, a precise historical reason for its vulnerability to outside predators and for the indifferent, almost embarrassed, quality of its civic spirit. As late as 1875, when it was already one of the three most beautiful large urban areas in Britain, Edinburgh and Bath being the other two, Cheltenham was still petitioning for a mayor and corporation against the contemptuous opposition of its upper classes. From that quite recent social rift over the relevance of democracy it has never completely recovered.

During the resultant Government Inquiry, James Winterbotham, a fierce opponent of the petition, questioned Baron de Ferrieres, the accepted leader of the town's society. The following exchange resulted:

Winterbotham:
What is the feeling of the Upper Class in Cheltenham with regard to Incorporation and what do you think its effects will be on the Town?
Baron:
I think that to introduce into it a certain number of people who could claim official precedence,

including their wives and daughters, would be to throw an apple of discord into it and would be injurious to the town. It must be borne in mind that we have no Merchants, no Manufacture, only Trade. It might be said that the Mayor and Aldermen would not wish to intrude into the balls, but I think they would stand up for their rights.
Winterbotham:
You think the ladies would look upon it with apprehension?
Baron:
I think they would.

So, against the wishes of this social élite, which had ruled previously through a body of Commissioners, Cheltenham was incorporated with a mayor and aldermen in 1876. The Baron became, from a sense of noblesse oblige, the town's second mayor and left his picture collection to found an art gallery but, disenchanted with the new regime of trade, the old

The Imperial Spa, first built where the Queen's Hotel now stands, was moved to the corner of St George's Road and The Promenade in 1838.

upper-class drifted elsewhere. Since that time it has never been fashionable to love Cheltenham, only to enjoy it, mock it, or make money ravaging it. One of the handsomest towns in Europe has inspired curiously little civic loyalty and the Baron's replies to James Winterbotham go some way towards explaining that frigidity. Under the old Commissioners a society of gentry and trade, with no history or traditions worth mentioning, had come together for high living and profit. This was succeeded after the reforms of 1876 by a new population of liberal minded educators, machine-part mechanics and professional spies. The political administrators whom they voted into existence have been trying ever since to make sense of the infrastructure they inherited: a long, undistinguished High Street, five aristocratic suburbs planned like classical elysiums and four artisan areas of much charm but isolated by sharp architectural boundaries. The place exuded class distinctions without offering a single stately home which people could grow fond of, look up to for historic continuity or pay to enter on guided tours. Even anecdotal history was meagre. Byron came here to complain snobbishly of the company and compare the town, inexplicably, to Inverness. Tennyson arrived to be draped in cold wet blankets for several months hoping to cure his melancholia, only to write the most desolate love poem in the language, *In Memoriam*.

Inevitably in the following pages the record of past and present councillors and their advisers will be criticised harshly. What should be said here, before that attack begins, is that Cheltenham presents and has presented an exceptionally difficult problem in survival. It was designed for a leisured class, which will never return, in order for them to drink water which is valueless if not

One notable rescue. Normandy House, shown as Segrave House on the Merrett map, has been restored with exemplary care.

indeed actually tainted. Unfortunately for its present guardians it was built with a careless grace of flowering trees and painted stucco: several square miles of casual elegance and imaginative improvisations. It is a national treasure on an embarrassing scale, undeniably beautiful and desperately vulnerable because a good half of that beauty is a green vacancy of garden and trees. In this country we expect garden cities to be designed for deserving workers and an appreciative lower middle class. But it is shamelessly apparent that Cheltenham was a garden designed for the selfish rich, its spas an excuse for balls and entertainments every night, for revelry while the nation sank into post-1815 depression or struggled with industrial deprivation. 'We will make a journey to Cheltenham,' says Mr Bulstrode in *Middlemarch*. 'There are great spiritual advantages to be had in that town, along with the air and the waters, and six weeks there will be very refreshing for us.'

The Problem of Topography

Cheltenham was prodigal in its use of land because it began its spa life as a summer resort. Bath was more a winter spa, urban, stony, tightly planned against the weather. In Cheltenham, everything from the beginning was alfresco. Its first healing well was sited a good quarter of a mile south of the long east-west axis of the High Street and linked to the parish church not by lodging houses but by a Well Walk of rural elms. After the first Royal Crescent had been built in tame imitation of Bath, the new resort found its own informal building pattern for summer entertaining. Small villa-palaces were thrown up on the cheap to make a deliberate show of affluence, their brick cores transformed by plaster and paint to defy grey skies with private sunshine. Set on those marshy meadows, land was cheap and each villa was surrounded by something between a park and a garden, with yews, holm oaks, deodar cedars, chestnuts, Lombardy poplars and beech. It was not a town of flowers, though a self-conscious Council has made it that in recent years; it was a town of trees, grass and villas. The Cheltenham that the Commissioners created was described by S. Y. Griffiths in 1826 as 'a bold speculation which ... laid out its terraces, its pleasure grounds, its attached enclosures, its plantations, walks and approaches worthy the environs of a palace': the ultimate realisation in Europe of Picturesque urban living.

Five suburbs were planted in the decades between 1815 and 1845. To connect them to the spas which gave a hint of purpose to a round of social amusement, wide promenades and pleasure grounds were not so much laid out as organically evolved. There was Pittville to the north of the High Street, Montpellier, Lansdown and the Park to the south; then last, grandest and most vulnerable, Bayshill. All were projected by nonentities who risked bankruptcy for profit and cut their costs by employing local builders and pattern books. In that brief building boom the only architect of national rank ever involved was John Buonarotti Papworth. Cheltenham's renaissance was all the more satisfying because it was essentially of lowland Gloucestershire.

Between northern Pittville and the southern four suburbs there has always been the mundane barrier of the High Street, Leland's 'longe towne havynge a Market'. A market, in fact, is what it has never satisfactorily produced. Resorts do not favour the undercutting of shop prices and Gloucester's thriving market only nine miles away has always been a disturbing element in Cheltenham's commercial awareness. The five aristocratic suburbs create a north-south axis across the High Street's east-west course but never confidently cross it, only hesitate on either side. This means that the town has no compact inner core for ring roads to circle at a safe distance. Excellence is

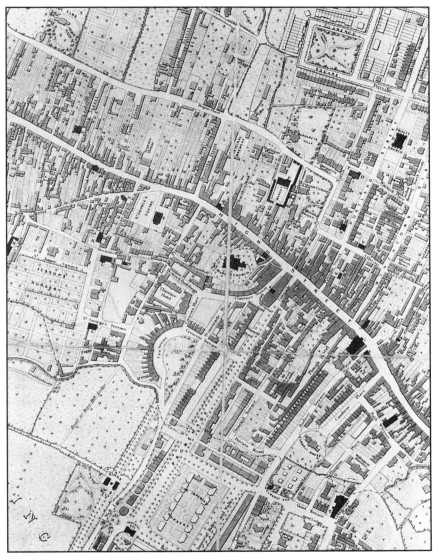

Merrett's Cheltenham map of 1834 illustrates the problems that would afflict the town over the next 150 years. The northern axis up Portland Street towards Pittville makes no connection across the east-west axis of the High Street with the southern axis down The Promenade. In the bottom right-hand corner are the tempting gardens on Vittoria Walk with Oriel Lodge and Lindsay Cottage, later Wolseley House. A little to the left is Broad Walk. The King's Well and Well Walk are now lost in the Ladies' College. Bayshill is still open fields.

inconveniently elongated and widespread. Over the nineteenth century the High Street developed three fine hotels, a Gothic Revival grammar school, an Assembly Room and an elegant gatehouse to a brewery. All have been demolished, so Cheltenham presents the planners' paradox of an old-fashioned centre that could be rebuilt without significant loss but with a long, relatively new, counter axis of two Regency peninsulas where literally nothing can be pulled down or cut down without lessening a unique whole.

First Casualties

Once it had achieved a mayor and corporation Cheltenham declined gently for the remainder of the nineteenth century. An actual slight drop in population meant a worrying decline in rates. When the income from its rates falls, the power and patronage of a municipal bureaucracy falls with it. Alarm bells ring and nervous councillors begin to look around for ways in which their town can be prostituted in order to attract more shoppers, more institutions and more investment. Beauty and a readiness to accommodate a client are always a harlot's most marketable assets.

The only serious building losses in these slack years before 1900 were the Doric portico of the Literary and Philosophical Institution on the Promenade, the richly pilastered Pump Room at the Royal Well, Bays Hill House, where George III had stayed in 1788, and an enchantingly frivolous Hindu entrance to the Market on High Street. All were indicators of the new borough's indifference to style, social meeting places and past history. More immediately threatening to the town's good looks was the settling of a cuckoo in the nest when Cheltenham Ladies' College moved in 1873 to its present site in Bayshill. One of the College's first acts of insensitive indifference to its responsibilities was the destruction of the superb Corinthian ballroom at the Old Well. This destroyed at a stroke that first Arcadian axis of the young spa, Well Walk. It also signalled an

The incoherent rock-faced facades of the Ladies' College down Montpellier Street cover Well Walk, the straight grove of trees shown on Merrett's map.

expansion that was to blight a whole strategic quarter of the town between Montpellier and Bayshill with ugly, pretentious buildings ill-related to each other and disastrously unrelated to the classical villas and terraces around them. Because it was the Ladies' College, an almost national institution, a pillar of the establishment and a symbol of moral righteousness, no one ever cared to point out that its visual manners were those of a vulgar plutocrat with a taste for fancy French detail and clumsy rock-faced masonry.

Two more signs of crass planning and lower expectations fell upon Imperial Square. This open space, which should be the key to the town's brilliant north-south axis, has always faltered in its growth, never more so than now when the town is still fumbling with the problem of completing a scheme begun 150 years ago. But back in 1873 the New Club was allowed to be built, a dim design error decently veiled in shrubs and trees on the titular Square's north-west corner. Most of the surviving open land, a nursery, was covered in 1878 by the Winter Gardens, a commercial venture intended to recharge the town's fading magnetism as a resort. Its virtue was its eccentricity and air of ponderous jollification; its vice was that it made the subsequent siting of a new Town Hall, adjacent to it in the middle of the wrecked 'Square', appear acceptable.

The Town Hall thrust its Edwardian baroque backside into the Square in 1900-3. So many much more insensitive insults have since been offered to Cheltenham's stylistic image that it is tempting to laugh off its design by Frederick Waller. To put a pompous Viennese entrance front in angry orange stone next to two fastidiously underplayed stucco terraces might be

The loutish rear elevations of the Town Hall with its attendant car-park destroy the open elegance of Imperial Square and flout the scale of the surrounding terrace.

In 1878 the Winter Garden was built on what Merrett's map shows as the Imperial Nursery. This opened the way to the disastrous siting of the Town Hall, just visible to the left, in 1900.

accepted as a one-off incident in a town of some architectural humour. But Waller's Town Hall is a large rectangular building and Waller designed it as if for a built-up city street with only one visible front. Like some nonconformist chapel raised on the cheap, its other three sides are clumsy, functional nondescripts, brazenly exposed inside a square of otherwise real distinction.

Bad taste is infectious. It was around the Town Hall that the demolitions and stylistic rot were to set in between the wars and there that the worst barbarisms have been inflicted in the post-war free-for-all. Another is impending over its south side in 1995. Yet as late as 1930, the broad area between the Bath Road on the east and Imperial Square and Montpellier Gardens to the west was one of complex beauty, with one elegant spa of 1804, twelve great villas, each a distinguished and distinct essay in Regency design, together with a charming scatter of period cottages and minor terraces. The whole was generously planted with trees and laid out in those all too tempting gardens.

Then Cambray House was pulled down and in its place rose Cambray Court flats: a large, brick-built block in the neo-Georgian style, higher than any of the surrounding buildings: living units for a new society where domestic servants were few and far between. In comparison with the tower blocks of the 1960s it has come to seem a cautious design with nervous period detail. Coldly appraised it is gross and thoughtless, a typical block of London flats, a lesser Dolphin Square transported from Thames-side with the wrong materials and with windows too small for a main mass too large. Built in a pleasant backwater off the High Street, it established a principle to which later planners, hard pressed, would turn in relief: 'If the thing looks Georgian pass it and let it be built.'

A more subtle and more threatening precedent was set when Suffolk House, the presiding element in Cheltenham's grandest complete enclosure, Suffolk Square, was demolished in 1935. Eric Cole designed the Suffolk House flats that replaced it, neither quite in nor out of Suffolk Square. No neo-Georgian uncertainties here but a modish Art Deco, sculpted by balconies, ingenious in its massing and approached by sub-

London building types arrive in mid-1930s Cheltenham – Cambray Court flats, genteel Georgian on an indigestible scale.

Suffolk House flats on Suffolk Square – ideal for Brighton, they replaced a large Regency house and its garden.

Saracenic porches. On any seaside between Brighton and Florida, Cole's creation would have been admirable. It exemplified the later claim taken up by journalists in the architectural press that a good contemporary building, architect designed, will look right in any context. The corollary to which is that a new design in an old style is wrong because it is a cheat, almost, in aesthetic terms, a sin.

The Suffolk House flats were an early instance of a trendy design offered for a prestigious site already beautiful with older buildings. The flats were a superior article aimed at middle income residents who would enjoy living in a superior area like Suffolk Square. So they broke the existing pattern of classical villa, classical terrace and proprietary chapel Gothick, broke the building line, the skyline and the traditional mix of stone and stucco. In a square where every domestic window was a vertical rectangle they flaunted the wrap-around horizontals of a Noel Coward roadhouse. It is a reasonably good building but an aesthetic parasite in absolutely the wrong place. In 1936 Cheltenham was still intact enough to absorb the shock, but the flats were a negative event.

Two years later the chalybeate Cambray Spa, an

Cambray Spa, an essential counterpoint to Oriel Lodge, was demolished in 1938 to make a wider, faster road.

enchanting octagon in full-blooded Perpendicular Gothic with a cavernous vaulted porch, was demolished to make a vacant space. Again the disease has proved infectious. Now Cheltenham is hollow with vacant spaces where there were once good buildings. Anything and everything is accepted in order to tempt the rich pickings of Cotswold shoppers and their Range Rovers away from the better bargains of Gloucester. But the Cambray octagon, which had latterly served as a Turkish Bath, was the most lyrical of the town's pump rooms. It had been built in 1834 as a deliberate visual counterpoint to the 1823 Oriel Lodge, diagonally across the road; it lay however in the blighted ambience of the Town Hall and in 1938 the voices of Betjeman and Piper had barely been recognised. So it went . Then, mercifully for Cheltenham's building stock, though for little else, war broke out, to be followed by a period of national destitution and a breathing space for a Regency spa town.

Vittoria Vandalised

In 1944, as the war was ending, Cheltenham Borough Council turned for advice on redevelopment and reconstruction of the town to that most genteel of conservation societies, the Georgian Group, which responded the next year with a measured 'Report on Cheltenham'. Nothing expresses the change that has afflicted local attitudes better than the contrast between that deferential gesture and the present Chief Executive's initiative in 1994, bringing in Reg Ward, recently the supremo of the ultra-modern commercial regeneration of London's Canary Wharf, not merely to make a report on the town's future which ignores Cheltenham's official 1991 Local Plan Review, but to become an actual executive servant of the borough projecting his own dynamic, divisive and deeply destructive vision of a new Cheltenham.

That earlier report from the Georgian Group was modest, sensible, but quite inadequate to the town's new circumstances. It listed the buildings worth preserving, studiously ignoring brilliant Italianate terraces like Lypiatt and York on St George's Road and implying by the list's mere existence that lesser excellences could be dispensed with. There was some further praise for wide roads and finally a disastrous recommendation that future buildings should be 'blocks of flats of simple form, three or four storeys in height'. Scale not style was the Georgian Group's concern and the dull council flats on Queen Elizabeth's Way should be seen as an eventual result of the report's urgings.

What the Group had not dared to say was that the town had already fatally wounded itself by doubling its population and that any further increase should be strenuously resisted.

Hindsight is, of course, easy, and in 1945 with the end of a victorious war, a baby boom and a Labour government, expansion was in the air and élitist aestheticism was unthinkable. But Cheltenham's real situation then was exactly the same as it is today: a population expanded beyond the ability of the infrastructure to carry it. The town's two environmental misfortunes had been the war-time prosperity of

Flats on the Gloucester Road – a dutiful attempt to follow the advice of the Georgian Group's 1945 report, but neither new nor convincing.

25

Dowtys and the permanent settlement in two spreading complexes of GCHQ. In 1935 Cheltenham's population was still only 50,000, not impossibly greater than its ideal level of 35,000 in 1850. But by 1950 it was at 80,000 and, with Cold War prosperity, the need for armaments and information, on the up and up.

Inevitably there was a rapid growth of council houses and flats, with some undistinguished private housing, all on an outer ring. This was the so-called 'doughnut effect', exaggerated in this case by the town's earlier lavish use of land. In 1935 the five upper class suburbs and the four harmonious artisan estates already covered between them six gracious square miles. All of these, except South Town which had developed its own shopping area, could be served without too much inconvenience of travelling by Cheltenham's very

Oriel Lodge of 1823 and its bad neighbours. Not a blade of grass survives from its once large garden on a key corner site.

circumscribed central shopping area: the long, narrow High Street for regular purchases and the Promenade, with far more trees than shops, for fashion and leisure. The post-war estates, lying outside this wide area of forbidden privilege, depended heavily on transport, on buses at first, but increasingly on private cars, for shopping and entertainment. Cars need parking spaces and the Council was under the additional pressure of knowing that these outer south-western estates – Benhall, St Mark's, Rowanfield and Hester's Way – could shop as easily or better in the rival twin city of Gloucester. That pressure would grow in the late-1960s when a fast, dual carriageway was driven through to link the two urban areas.

Gloucester, in the latter half of this century, has been Cheltenham's evil genius. If Cheltenham had been content with a 50,000 population it could have remained what it had been laid out, planted and built, to be: a garden town, an art-and-leisure residential complex, cosseted and cared for as a national treasure like a larger Ludlow or Warwick. Instead its attractive, establishment image, that leafy lure which brought GCHQ to Cheltenham rather than to Gloucester, began to destroy it. Dowtys, to give the firm its due, had moved out in 1935 to invisible premises at Arle Court. The real vultures, the insurance companies and national utilities, moved eagerly into the most sensitive sections of a town that offered elegant prestige headquarters ready built and going cheap, and where housing costs for their staff were much lower than in London.

The first and most ruthless vandalism, on this side of outright demolition, fell on Oriel Lodge. Perhaps it was its extra wide garden, perhaps its nearness to the town centre, perhaps in the 1950s Gothick as opposed to classical was still considered fair game. Whatever the reasons, its fate has been dramatic. Sold as early as

1931 to General Accident Insurance, that wide green lawn and those mature trees became irresistible. Two uncompromisingly utilitarian blocks were built close to Edward Jenkins's playfully poetic facades of 1823 and every last inch of grass was covered in tarmac. The Lodge now stands like a parody of commercial greed sketched by Osbert Lancaster to illustrate the soulless Philistines at their worst.

Worse was to come, and as usual in such development, lightning struck again in the same place. As if preparing consciously for the final, unbelievable, architectural outrage – the thirty-storey Eagle Star office tower – developers and demolition men began to soften up the area around it, concentrating on Vittoria Walk. Two of the town's finest classical villas, Wolseley House and Farnley Lodge that had faced each other superbly, one on either side of the Walk, were demolished or obliterated. Both had large gardens and on the long finger of winding paths and greenery that Wolseley

It is easy to imagine how daring the graceless finger of stained concrete looked on the original architect's drawings. Wolseley's giant Ionic order puts the vaunted simplicities of modernist design into perspective.

Wolseley Terrace before it lost its canopies and became enclosed in the dim back yard of a Post Office building. (Crown Copyright RCHME).

Wolseley Terrace decanopied and sunless in its new back yard.

House had extruded down to Wolseley Terrace an outstandingly graceless, two-storey concrete arm on thin stilts, was built by the telephone branch of the Post Office. This, at a stroke, left Wolseley Terrace with its giant order of deeply fluted Corinthian pilasters and cream-painted stucco stripped of its intended veil of trees, confronted by concrete pavements and stained concrete slabs.

This ruined area is valuable in just one sense. It is easy here to envisage how bold, modern and attractive the draughtsman's drawings must have looked when the appropriate Council committee passed them. The lines are exciting; the reality is drab and destructive. Ideally Wolseley House should have been turned into a small condominium – there would have been no shortage of residents – and its gardens protected. But if these bad new buildings have to be retained, their ransom should be the twentieth century equivalent of a stucco dressing and a fresh coat of paint every ten years. Written into the Council's policy for new building within the Conservation Area should be: 'Concrete is inexcusable, reconstructed stone is a sham, brick is only allowed for contextual reasons, Cotswold stone is passable, stucco is perfect.' Cheltenham lives and glows by its stucco. Stucco is expensive in upkeep. Therefore entrepreneurs who cannot afford stucco should not be allowed to build within the sacred six square miles.

Ashley House in the blighted environs of the Town Hall.

Ellenborough House – regularity, bland economy of construction and a potent magnet for commuters' cars in Cheltenham's gutted centre.

The High Street Falls Unnoticed

While Cheltenham High Street was never one of the great shopping streets of Britain, it took the town only five years in the middle 1960s to turn it into one of the most unattractive. That was a thrusting time when the despised suffix of 'Spa' was being lopped off 'Cheltenham' and a brave new future of something else, that no one was exactly sure about, was being trumpeted by a Conservative majority Council, one of whose members was soon to be the town's Conservative MP.

Depending upon whether it was approached from London or from Tewkesbury, the High Street took a traveller up or down the architectural class system. Coming in on the London Road the impact was impressive with villas and gardens on the left, wide lawns and regular stone terraces with fine ironwork on the right. Facing up the road at right-angles was an almost indecently grand town house, The Priory, with a giant Corinthian order, the kind of status symbol any self-respecting town would normally venerate. Then, still with wide open vistas of grass, ironwork and low-sweeping cedars on the right, the scene became more urban and there was an elegant Regency hotel, the Bellevue, giving exactly the right note of light-hearted welcome to a town of resort.

After that there came, if not anti-climax, a certain lowering of tension, a narrowing of the street, a lack of vista. A slimmed-down Assembly Room had long ago been replaced by a fattened-up Lloyds Bank. But then on the right there was a building sequence of real provincial merit: a handsome classical gatehouse to a brewery, an imposing Victorian Gothic grammar school with a turret and statues of its benefactors, finally a large Georgian hotel, The Fleece, conventionally regular in its proportions. These three, standing side by side, were the street furniture that most towns would value. Thereafter, via St George's underplayed square, the High Street faded into a likeable straggle of rundown public houses, side alleys and cottages.

First to fall, in the mid-1960s, were the street's best three buildings, the sequence around the Grammar School. Even now anyone familiar with the street has to blink and think twice before accepting that buildings so reasonably fine could have been replaced by anything as unbelievably bad – not weak, not dull, but actively bad, even aesthetically crippled – as the Sainsbury block which replaced them. Sainsbury and Tesco have built many interesting stores in other towns but their Cheltenham shops are a disaster, a mindless irregularity that lurches threateningly over the pavement on

The Priory, demolished for an office block in 1967.

concrete crutches that were, apparently, unable to carry even such a slight mass and have had to be given extra support before they were twenty years old. The building is an extreme instance of what, in the brazen 1960s, a respectable planning committee would allow and two rich grocery chains utilise on a prime site. In time, the building could attract a preservation order as an interesting nadir of English taste.

While this strange addition to a devalued street was going up, quietly, ignoring a little polite protest, The Priory was coming down. Its replacement, Mercia House, is bland and characterless. Why The Priory's splendid stone shell could not have been retained to front an office interior has not been explained. Ignorant indifference in the town's governing class could be the reason. If the cost of preservation and internal reconstruction would have been too high for the developers, they should have been told to go elsewhere. A pattern of undervaluing the town's assets and attractions was setting in. There is no real evidence yet that the pattern has been broken.

The Grammar School as it fronted the High Street. A corner of the handsome Regency gatehouse to the brewery can be seen to the left. (Crown Copyright RCHME).

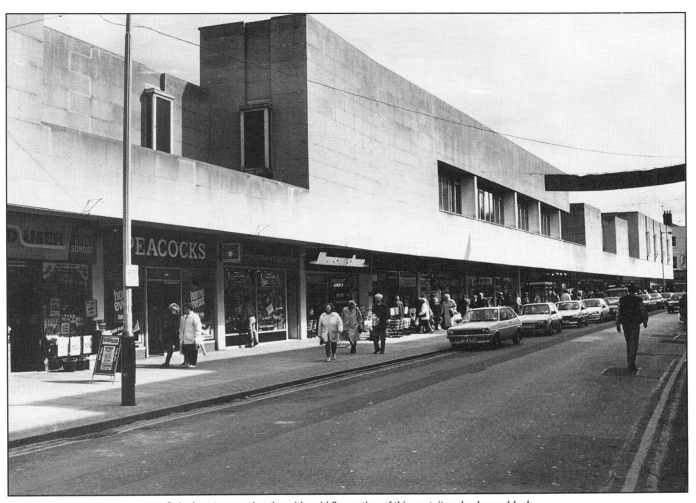

Sainsbury's occupies the wide middle section of this gratuitously clumsy block where the Fleece and the Grammar School gave character to the High street until 1966.

All Roads South

These late 1960s and early 1970s were vintage years for the developers in Cheltenham. This was the time when it was easy to pull down a fine building on a visually strategic site, replace it with something cheap and nondescript, yet still expect a verbal pat on the back from the local press, *The Gloucestershire Echo*. This paper, unlike its sister to the south, *The Bath Evening Chronicle*, played and plays a generally supine role in the town's steady self-destruction, faithfully echoing the estate agents' language of mild delight at each new proposal for ruin. While the Bath paper runs a regular, weekly critical feature on local architectural proposals, the *Echo* appears to believe that its readers would not be interested. If it is good for trade and employment then it must be good for Cheltenham. This line of pavement politics still rules the town.

Cavendish House on the Promenade is the undisputed sun king of the town's shopping. It was established in 1826 and until 1964-6 possessed of a fruity Edwardian shop-front, a richly carved ornament to the wide axial street on which it stands. By 1966 ghastly good taste, as Betjeman understood it, had taken over with a complete reconstruction of discreetly panelled Cotswold stone. A little further down the Promenade something much worse was going on. The New Club had never been an addition to a street both noble, subtle and unexpected, but at least it looked like a house and was largely concealed by trees. In the 1960s the trees were felled, the club was demolished and a wonderfully clever exercise in understated overuse of a site took its place: the Quadrangle building. Even now it is rarely mentioned as the visual offence which it undoubtedly is, so regular and discreet is its articulation in tactful response to the Regency's supposed restraint, so irreproachable the muted colouring of its stone fascia. That it blocks out what should be the sudden unfolding of Imperial Square is never mentioned. Surrounded by villas alive with imaginative invention and backed by the St Petersburg pomp of the Queen's Hotel, it offers nothing itself except a tactful near-invisibility like that

Possibly the most ingeniously destructive modern addition to Cheltenham's streets, the Quadrangle is so unassuming and tedious that no one bothers to hate it despite the visual block which it offers to a green park.

The ABC cinema in tactful pastiche Georgian replaced in 1937 the old Imperial Spa building at the end of the terrace on The Promenade.

The inverted black glass pagoda that over-confident architects offered as a replacement for the ABC cinema.

As it turns a corner, the confident Progressive Classicism of Royscot House begins to falter, phasing into two graceless blocks that affront Royal Crescent.

Royscot House, a wise solution to a controversial site. This building of 1985 is stylistically several decades older than the real 1825 terrace which it adjoins, but the solecism works admirably.

of Father Brown's murderous postman in the G. K. Chesterton story.

Across the way on another of the town's key positions is Royscot House: a far more exciting compromise between commercial profit and responsible development. When the ABC cinema standing at this south-west end of the noble municipal terrace was to be demolished the first modish proposal, for an admittedly testing site, was for an inverted pagoda of glass and steel, Cheltenham's answer to downtown Dallas. This was howled down in one of those rare upsurges of civic spirit that tend to leave the town drained for the next decade. What was then proposed, accepted and built was Royscot, an undeniably handsome and competent evocation of an early Palladian building. Six Doric columns make a fair show of supporting its austere facade. It looks expensive but tasteful, as indeed it is: solid proof that when the planning committee of one of the most beautiful, and therefore desirable, urban complexes in Britain sticks its heels in it can command anything from an eager developer.

Unfortunately those councillors and their planning officers were not confident enough. Royscot is a typical compromise of the 1980s. Around the corner from this Palladian front a price has been paid. The hinder parts of the building are two louche, rectangular blocks, linked by black glass and squeezing the maximum permitted use from the site. Indifferent to the Royal Crescent which they face, they do nothing for a blighted town space which they could have rescued.

Visible from this point up St George's Road is the far more wholesale visual vandalism of the late 1950s. The Magistrates' Court, a neurotic flutter of concrete fins between forty identical metal window bays, is set above a large gaping car-park that manages to reveal all the graceless infill that has been crammed in behind the

The dreadful backsides of Bayshill. These greedy infills behind St George's House are one side of the ugly open space that has been hacked out to provide parking for the dreary Magistrates' Court.

The Magistrates' Court on St George's Road. Concrete fins were a cliché of the 1960s. This car-park exposes the uninspired rear of Elizabeth House on Parabola Road.

villas on Parabola and Bayshill Roads. It is probably the worst instance of ugly design and tactless clearance in the town. On the opposite side of the road, York Terrace and the surviving Ionic portico of the original three on St George's Terrace half redeem the wreck.

A handsome new entrance to the Ladies' College required the demolition of a Samuel Onley villa.

Linotype Hell, the twentieth century's response to the delicate nineteenth century Gothic of Cheltenham Gentlemen's College across the road.

At the corner by the Neptune fountain, three roads lead off towards the south and west, with a fourth, the Bath Road, two blocks away. Until 1950 all four were lined with villas and trees in a display of picturesque urban design without equal in Britain. Even now the Promenade, despite the blight of the Quadrangle, is an unpredictable visual pleasure, but all the other three – St George's Road, Bayshill Road and the Bath Road – have been desperately wounded under the eyes of a planning department. The wreck of St George's has been described, the first half of Bayshill on its east side has been ruined by the Ladies' College and all the west side villas mutilated or demolished. As for the Bath Road, its entire length is now dominated by the thirty storeys of the Eagle Star tower, and next to that extraordinary usurpation two graceless rectangularities, the Linotype Hell and the Midland Bank buildings, outface the Gothic and Greek Revival ranges of Cheltenham College with the raw assurance of criminals who knew that the jury would be asleep.

A Visionary Tower

The Eagle Star tower, perhaps the ultimate triumph of job creation over intelligent planning procedures.
The restoration of Eagle House, dwarfed in the foreground, would have been seen as a planning gain in 1968.

The Eagle Star building has been so much, and so rightly, abused and ridiculed that it is worth spending as much time on its implications for local government in a

Broad Walk, beyond the Queen's Hotel, has been an unresolved problem of development for almost two centuries. It is now threatened with over building. As usual the Eagle Star tower intrudes upon the scene.

sleeping town as on its physical actuality. To be brief, it is 200 feet and thirty storeys high, an irregular octagon mottled in colour contrasts of prefabricated panels. There is sub-Aztec decoration, of the kind that shrewdly defies critical analysis, on its crown and around its base. From near and far it wrecks Cheltenham. Three villas and their gardens were flattened to give it room to rise. Two other villas have been preserved to testify to the insurance firm's basic warm heart.

It appears that even Eagle Star now regards its construction as a mistake and was, before a recent programme of renovation, considering the alternative of demolition. A central lift core is now desperately unfashionable in architectural circles and the tower's solid flooring is unfunctional for sophisticated computer wiring. The firm is now tactfully dispersing its whole operation about the town in lower, less offensive structures. So perhaps, in another ten years, there may be some positive demolition.

What is so important now is to absorb the lesson which this dreadful tower still teaches about the nature of local government in a democratic town. If a project is monstrous enough to catch the public imagination, local politicians will go for it with panic street politics about unemployment, the need for 'vision', for social regeneration, for confronting the twenty-first century and all that tired rubbish that television producers and press barons deploy to keep us awake in our armchairs. Then, when the election is over and the damage is becoming apparent, there are several more years for forgetfulness to seep in before the polls open again and a new hare has to be started.

The Eagle Star tower went up while the country was still bathing in Harold Wilson's 'white heat of the new technology'. Otherwise, even Cheltenham might have said, 'No!' Now, when Reg Ward and the town's Chief

Executive are projecting a new 'vision thing' – social regeneration for St Paul's and a linear business park all the way from the St James's station site to the old gasworks – it is helpful to remember the Eagle Star tower and those two gloomy hulks of office building already stranded on Jessop Avenue. They are ugly in themselves, the absolute antithesis of 'vision', and they do not merely increase the traffic problem, they actually create that problem. Without the influx of commuters that they and their kind generate, Cheltenham's roads could cope comfortably. Visionary tower blocks are themselves the traffic problem. When the Eagle Star went up, London was busily destroying its own skyline so Cheltenham had some slight excuse. In these more disenchanted days, local authorities might consider the moral courage required to project negative growth and to tell harsh economic truths to a lazy and ill-informed electorate.

In the past Conservative council majorities presided over Cheltenham's visual decline. There is no sign that the present Liberal Democrat majority has learnt from blunders like the Eagle Star tower. Each newly elected idealist appears to wilt before official advice, long briefs to be mastered, and pressures from the press to offer phoney solutions. The south side of Imperial Gardens, along the Broad Walk and next to the Queen's Hotel, is the obvious site for a modest residential development, three villas or a short terrace, delicately detailed and veiled by mature trees. Extensions to Montpellier Spa Road and a villa pair proposed for Priory Road by the Guilor Petch partnership prove that both Scholarly Reproduction and Progressive Classicism have come of age in Cheltenham. Good design, thoughtful of context, is available.

Yet the Council's planning committee has acted with nervous irresolution when confronted with a fat, greedy office development for this most sensitive site on Imperial's Broad Walk. As usual, when cubic feet and high rentals are the prize, both aesthetic and environmental causes are ignored.

Vultures in Villas and on the Garden Trees

Fifty or more miniature palaces once made Cheltenham unique. The town was the ultimate artefact of the Picturesque movement, Romantic not Roman. Its classical and Gothick structures were set out in deliberate confusion about a planned forest of trees; it was a spa in the mood of Richard Payne Knight and Uvedale Price. Since 1930 these villas have suffered terribly. Wolseley, Abbeyholme, Montpellier Place, Cranley, Elmfield, Rosehill, Ashfield, Eamont, Pery Lodge, The Priory, Cambray, Suffolk, Rock Cottage and Farnley are all gone and some twenty others have been desperately mauled by their supposed rescuers.

'Quality of life' has been the lure. Cheltenham is in the West Country; the Cotswolds hang over it like a wave that never breaks. The town has a theatre, a music and literary festival, a famous race course. Royalty live near and the best shops appear to stand in green parks. When a commercial firm or a utility wants to attract a stable work-force to perform its often rather tedious and repetitive office routines, it is always a help if it can offer 'quality of life' in addition to a modest salary.

What happens is that the vultures fly in, find a gently dilapidated villa, inhabited perhaps by a few old people or used as a run-down hotel. There may be dry rot in the attic, cracks in a side wall and the stucco is peeling. So it is a conservation problem and a concern to those officials paid to be concerned.

John Middleton's Gothic masterpiece, Abbeyholme, with a workman smashing its stonework. Museums moved in to cherish portions of this house which Cheltenham demolished without a second thought (Cheltenham Borough Council).

An offer is made. No expense will be spared. There will be a new roof, permitting additional floor space in a mansard attic, complete treatment for the woodwork

Sovereign House on Bayshill Road is a very recent example of a greedy and inappropriate infill executed in notably thin token pastiche. No attempt was made to respond to its Italianate parent house.

morning; another large Cheltenham garden is lost and a villa that once stood in leafy isolation has its fine lines confused by messy additions in the wrong materials. The garden town will be that much less itself.

and, of course, a fresh coat of paint in the original colours of 1835 as detected by an expert from paint scrapes. There must, however (the reservation is slipped in), be planning permission for thirty car-parking spaces on the gardens hidden, in part at least, by shrubs; and there will have to be a large extension at the rear for canteen, kitchen and typing pool. For that, a sympathetic design is offered, not quite in the style of the main house, but then an exact copy would be dishonest. Tourists might think that they were looking at a Regency typing pool and that would never do. So something in a more modern idiom and, naturally, in modern materials, but Regency in its essential simplicity, or so it is suggested, is agreed.

That, more or less, is how the bargaining has gone on. To satisfy the conservation section an extra string course may be added to the plans for the extension to bind the composition together. Everyone is satisfied. A business rate will be paid for the extended premises; the new office staff will have their 'quality of life' somewhere out in Charlton Kings. So the roads into town become a crawl of commuters every weekday

Vandalised and empty, Regan House stands at the end of Lansdown Terrace.

After all, the word goes around, the house was in a very poor state. It was the only way to save it.

But was it? That is the question that must not be shirked. Is rescue at the price of architectural mutilation and garden devastation the only way? Cheltenham has its terraces, one of them – Lansdown – the most dramatic in Britain: an erratic cliff hung like Babylon with columned balconies and tragic in decay; but the town's glory is its villas. They present that variety of invention that makes Cheltenham greater in its parts if lesser as a whole than Bath, and they are going.

All the demolished villas could have been saved and all the mutilated ones left in their original condition if the Borough Council had, from the start, refused permission for anything except conversions into flats and condominiums. The villas, centrally placed, surrounded by attractive gardens, admirably proportioned in their rooms, would never have been short of tenants. As the Georgian Group report of 1945 pointed out, 'the problem of conversion is easier in that only the facades require strict conservation and the interiors can be freely modelled where necessary'.

There would, of course, be a penalty. Their rates would be lower than business rates. The price of safeguarding the 'garden town' would be a higher council rate burden for everyone fortunate enough to live in it and enjoy its 'quality of life'. The advantages would be fewer traffic movements between the outer 'doughnut ring' and the inner Regency suburbs, with a consequent improvement in air quality. Finally the Borough Council would have to make the logical decision to site all firms wishing to move into the town out on the flat fields to the west of the outer residential ring. If those firms then decided on another town, so much the better. Negative growth is a positive virtue: bad for house agents, good for residents. If Cheltenham's population ceased to grow or even

Tudor Lodge, designed by Samuel Daukes as his own home, was demolished in 1968, one of many losses on The Park.

Tudor Lodge's banal replacement.

slightly declined that should be welcomed, not made the panic exercise for councillors to prove their political machismo by hyping up a disastrous development scheme. When electors hear of exciting new schemes for progress and prosperity they should look carefully

An example of parody infill next to an authentic villa on Parabola Road.

and leisure services, once called out in a council meeting: 'For God's sake stand still!'

For conservation there is no substitute for an alert citizen, preferably one born in the town and possessed of a keen eye.

The villas of Cheltenham have come in for five distinct treatments: demolition, parody, brutalization, furtive concealment and thoughtful response. Some of the demolitions have been particularly distressing. As recently as 1992 Papworth's Rosehill, which still retained painted ceilings and later, fine Victorian Rococo plasterwork, was levelled. Abbeyholme on Overton Road, a pre-Raphaelite villa by the church architect John Middleton, was of such quality that the Bowes Museum eagerly snapped up one of its ceilings, and other fittings went to America, when the house was replaced by a housing association complex.

Then, in this heavily ruined area of Overton Road, Elmfield went for a graceless tangle of concrete flats.

around them at what they have already: one of Europe's most attractive towns, and ask, 'whose progress and whose prosperity?' As one Bath councillor, in despair at the self-interested hyperactivity of that city's planners

This overmantel of Pre-Raphaelite tiles gives some impression of the quality of Abbeyholme before its senseless demolition.

Pery Lodge stood where the dreadful Magistrates' Court now flouts the laws of decent aesthetics. Eamont was where the Christian Science church lounges in a style quite inappropriate to Bayshill Road alongside the vacant grounds of demolished Ashfield. Tudor Lodge has gone from The Park; Montpellier Place is the mere foundations to the Eagle Star tower. Most gruesome of all is the fate of Farnley Lodge. Its Italianate tower is still just visible above the haphazard bits of brick and concrete that the YMCA in Vittoria Walk has gathered around it. So it hangs like a deer's head, undigested from the mouth of an over-ambitious boa constrictor.

Brutalization can take several forms. Those long neo-Georgian red brick arms flung out on either side of the

Elegant in itself, the Christian Science church makes no attempt to match the villa mood of Bayshill Road.

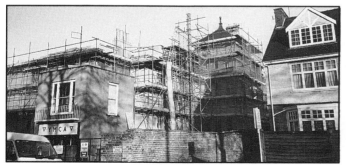

Farnley Lodge with its Italianate turret now lost in later accretions.

chaste white stucco of Bayshill Court have a charm of the confidently gauche. The governors of the Ladies' College, whose sanitorium it is, must have congratulated themselves that even if the Black Death returned to town their girls would die in classical wards. True brutalism is demonstrated by the National Westminster's premises added to No.2 Park Place, as inexcusable in its minor scale as the Eagle Star tower. Tucked away shamefully in a garden it could be ignored. Instead it rumbles along Suffolk Road hitting its decent Doric villa at cornice height without any effort to respond to storeys, style, materials or roof-scape. If its design team could explain to a public meeting what pressures they were under and what precisely they thought they were achieving, it could be recorded for an instructive half hour programme on Channel Four.

At the lower end of Bayshill Road the two treatments, brutalization and parody, are on show. This cross-roads with two terraces and three villas was, before development set in, one of the grandest concentrations of inventive classicism, an area that could, in its casual pomp, be compared with some of the finest urban

The Ionic pilasters of Fauconberg Lodge shackled to a shoddy extension of greenish units.

The National Westminster's premises of crude concrete and glass panels shame the refined lines of this Papworth villa on Park Place.

Arrogant infill – National Westminster House from another angle.

spaces in Europe. The Ladies' College has shackled the Ionic pilasters of Fauconberg Lodge to a shoddy extension of greenish prefabricated units, cement strip and render. As a distraction across the road, St George's House has been created to house the administration of Kraft cheese and foodstuffs. This has been done by taking the resoundingly porticoed Milverton Hotel and its quieter neighbour, both stucco-clad, and linking their vertical fenestration by a bold, four-storey block of horizontal fenestration on thin stilts, all in artificial stone.

A little way up Bayshill Road are some of the greediest garden infills of the town, parody extensions all the more cruel because the villas they mock – Bayshill House, De La Bere House, The Limes and Hadley House – carry some of the most adventurous and impressive Greek Revival experiment in England. At Hadley, the parody extension even goes underground to exploit the last ounce of garden soil.

The superb Ionic confidence of Bayshill House with its inevitable dressing of parked cars; the mews lane behind is an architectural black hole.

On Lypiatt Road there is a spectacular display of beggar-my-back-neighbour. To the front, four, severe, stone villas present Ionic and Doric porticoes that could stand as pure examples of the best neo-classicism, half-veiled with funereal evergreen trees. Their backs to Southwood Lane are a jungle of disorganised concrete blocks and prefabricated units, a visual slum that the inhabitants of Suffolk Square west side must face every morning. But if you are part of the national health authorities there are apparently no limits to what you can pack into a one-time garden.

At Sydney Lodge up Overton Road, what were once very large gardens have been utilized to vanishing point. To the west of the house a large semi-sunken extension lurks behind a high brick wall, while to the east there is a new block, more commonplace than brutal, but totally indifferent to the style of Baron de Ferrieres' house that adjoins it. Here, where King George III once stayed and set Cheltenham on the map of health and fashion, the spirit of the Regency has been diluted past perception.

Villa treatment by thoughtful response was promised, but an account of it has to be very brief. Across the road from Sydney Lodge is a refined but subdued villa of

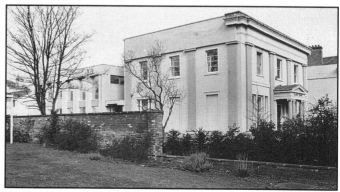

Hadley House on Bayshill Road – a prime example of infill by parody.

To its front on Lypiatt Road, Burlington House is austere and Doric.

To their rears on Southwood Lane, Burlington House and its neo-Classical neighbours have covered their gardens with mannerless infill.

The front lawns of The Beeches and Stratford House on Suffolk Square are a reminder of the lost Arcadian spa town.

Hill Samuel (once Carswell) on Parabola, Fullwood Park, Vittoria House, Marchmont, Oakhurst, Merrowdown, Eildon and Glenower may have been liberal with the tarmac but at least the structures survive intact. One amazing pair of semis on Suffolk Square – The Beeches and Stratford House – should be given a civic award and freed from council tax for five years. They have not only kept their fabric inviolate but also their green lawns, unkempt reminders of an Arcadian town almost forgotten. Then if there were any aesthetic justice, a particularly heavy council tax would be laid on the development which has taken place on the garden of Rhoderick Villa on the opposite side of the same square. Suffolk Mews, as this tight little group in brown brick and artificial stone contemporary vernacular is called, deserves a wooden spoon at least for being discreetly concealed from the square, but blatantly exposed and completely out of character at the back where Rhoderick's garden once ran up to Suffolk Road and Suffolk Parade. It was an area of unpretentious white houses, neighbourly and attractive, that could and should have inspired Suffolk Mews with the same good qualities. Until the committees which pass such developments have walked the contexts and absorbed the local idiom, nothing will go well.

creamy stucco, Upton Leigh. Very recently a sizeable addition, in effect an extra house, has been added to the side of it in precisely the same colour, roof slope, cornice, window architraves and flat string courses. It is a masterpiece of tact. Whether the gentle hilltop on which it sits is any better for this extra burden is open to question, but it is a demonstration of how well such things can be done if the money is spent.

To end with a roll, if not of honour, at least of modest praise, some villas have been treated with some respect.

Cheltenham's planners should surely have obliged the architect to respond to —

— the Regency streetscape across the road.

The Northern Relief Road — Relief or Ruin?

Names can conceal destructive realities. The Northern Relief Road, on which the town's traffic engineers have spent much of the town's time and what meagre finance they were allowed, is neither 'Northern' nor a 'Relief'. It is a spasmodic, half-built, arterial road directing traffic through the very middle of the town centre in, not one, but two routes. These routes not only divide the town into two or three parts, but spread visual squalor on either side as they bisect Cheltenham. Finally, after all this expense, noise, air pollution and inconvenience, this Northern Ruin Road leaves the High Street not quiet and pedestrianised, as might be expected, but still plagued for long stretches by a flood of cars.

To any detached observer it is obvious that the town should have concentrated its resources twenty years ago on a relief road far to the south on the route of the old Cirencester railway line, then through Leckhampton and Chargrove to the M5. This would have taken the east-west lorries and tourist traffic to Wales out of the town completely. But possibly because of fear, fear lest a single potential customer should be carried past the town's shops or a single guest whisked away from Cheltenham's hotels, this real Relief Road, an Outer Southern Relief Road, has never been built. The so called Northern Relief route, either along Swindon, St Margaret's and Fairview Roads or, with even more architectural sickness, along the alternative of Albion Street, is the result. Yet another route for entrapped lorries grinds to the south, through some of the town's richest and most valuable building stock along Thirlestaine Road and Suffolk Road.

The sheer incompetence and spreading ugliness of the Northern Relief has to be experienced to be believed. To lure the frustrated motorist it has occasional stretches of dual carriageway with a central reservation and easy, open curves to impel drivers into inappropriate speeds. These change abruptly to three lanes, then down to two grudging lanes cramped between brewery buildings.

They made a vacancy and called it a Relief Road – visual squalor now cuts Cheltenham into segments and encourages visitors to escape.

*The Northern Relief Road has blighted everything which it touches. The three low pyramids
in the foreground are modern Quaker architecture, a Friends' Meeting House.*

Writing in *Country Life* in November 1982, Michael Wright prophesied that the road would be a disaster, urging that 'its environmental impact is kept to the minimum by landscaping and that it does not irrevocably sever the northern part of the town from the High Street'. The Borough Engineer, constrained by lack of money from the County Council, has failed to landscape anything except Tom Price Close and has allowed Pittville and Fairview with their lakes, bridges and enchantingly varied villas, to be severed 'irrevocably' from the main town. Only an agile adolescent can cross the concentrated traffic stream at any point except the rare, light-controlled pedestrian crossings with central refuges.

By a perverse logic planners have allowed this dual route, where most travellers experience Cheltenham, to

Drivers on the Northern Relief Road get this impression of Regency Cheltenham.

The new red sorting office on the Relief Road.

Regency builders marked the union of a minor road with a major one by a note of heightened architecture. This pub was one such but now stands isolated in the Relief Road's blight –

– while twentieth century Cheltenham marks such a union by demolition and a blank wall.

be lined with new buildings of a jazzy vulgarity that would never be permitted on the town's ordinary streets. The Texas Homecare store, a giant scarlet and blue sausage straight out of USA commercialism, sets the tone on the Relief's outer strand. Where there are not wire fences and parking lots there are gaping repair shops brightly painted and the new Royal Mail office

which is built partly of red brick and partly of garish flowerpot-red metal units. When Regency builders were laying out St Paul's and Fairview they signalled the end of each minor road when it came to a major road by a note of heightened architectural ornament on shop, pub or end house. It is exactly these richer buildings that the Relief Road has vandalised, either knocking them down where money allowed or leaving them to fester in the blight of traffic noise and fumes. Lastly, where a wide, fast curve was created at the expense of Fairview, a brick baffle wall had to be built in an attempt to lessen the nuisance that the road engineers have created. Behind that a new suburb, Tom Price Close, has been built which wilfully ignores the humane, classical tradition of Fairview's white streets and subtle variety. It resorts instead to brown brick contemporary vernacular in standard units of two-storey houses and three-storey flats. The Department of the Environment advised in its recent *Quality in Town and Country* document that successful new buildings were 'those that unselfconsciously integrate into their contexts,

Contemporary Vernacular peeps over a sound baffle on a fast, easy curve of the Northern Relief.

Tom Price Close resolutely ignores the humane architectural idiom of Fairview.

Marks and Spencer's shameless brick backside on Albion Street, the town's visual no-go area and a second strand of the 'Relief' Road.

borrowing from local building techniques and using local materials'. Unfortunately the brown brick rash of Tom Price Close is all a passing motorist sees of Cheltenham's artisan suburbs, which at their best rival the famous barrios of Seville but no doubt infringe any number of directives about street frontages and ideal distances between 'units'.

From the raw brick wound where it leaves the Lower High Street, to the point where it throws a speeded-up traffic flow into the London Road by the cedars of Bellevue the Northern Relief Road is an unmitigated error in concept and in execution. When an Outer Southern Relief Road has finally been achieved in response to pressure from an informed electorate, much money will have to be spent building up the ruined sides of the Northern Relief with buildings in the town's native classical idiom. As for Albion Street, that inner alternative strand, exposed to Marks and Spencer's shameless brick backside, the slighted Coliseum, the tottering concrete modernism on Winchcombe Street, the sick-buff panels of Debenham's rear elevations and the brutalism of the Highbury Lane multi-storey car-park, Cheltenham must start again from scratch. It is all past praying for and how a town, desperate to attract shoppers to its charm and elegance, allowed such a congeries of visual depression to be built would make an interesting study in the philistinism of a democratically elected body.

The east side of Winchcombe Street was a coarse concrete attempt of 1965 to smarten up the town's shopping image in a curiously dated Lubetkin-style 1930s modernism. It appears to need support.

The west side of Winchcombe Street remains homely and various.

The sick-buff panels of Debenham's front on Albion Street relate to nothing else in the town – a typical modern 'one-off' and to hell with the rest.

A Sickness of Car-parks

It was interesting, though not in any way surprising, that when Colin Nye, Cheltenham's Chief Executive, invited an influential selection of borough and county councillors to come on a walkabout coach tour to boost Reg Ward's new plans for the town, literally three-quarters of his letter was spent in explaining how they could claim privileged parking places on the doorstep of the municipal offices. There was a large park for 800 cars only two blocks of a beautiful town away from those offices, a car-park incidentally that could be doubled in size if anyone cared, yet it was Colin Nye's automatic and almost certainly justified assumption that his guests would be either too self-important or too physically idle to walk those two beautiful blocks willingly. The car has corrupted and continues to corrupt us all. By their nature and by their appointment, neither Chief Executive nor councillors can resist, or even wish to resist, the pressures that determine the town's commercial viability and the power with which that will endow them. It is worth noting that Reg Ward's schemes for redeveloping Cheltenham contain hints that the parking problems of the Chief Executive might be solved in the future, though at a cost of £200 million.

In Transport Section 14 of the *Local Plan Review for Cheltenham Borough*, submitted in September 1991, there are 117 paragraphs and 116 of them brim with admirable analytical good sense. They anticipate every positive point and caution that wise traffic engineers could make, from relief roads, cyclists, rights, developers' responsibilities, to parking, public transport and light railways. But just one short paragraph, number 14.16, makes a gentle nonsense of the other 116. It reads: 'Motor vehicles make an important contribution to the economic vitality of the town and to restrict their use on a large scale would cause difficulties for the many shops and businesses.' That is the reality.

As long as this country permits the setting up and continuance of large out-of-town shopping centres with unlimited free parking there will be a senseless war between two sets of commercial interests. Old towns, desperate to compete, will tear their historic fabric apart as they open mediaeval streets or, in Cheltenham's case, a Regency Arcadia, to car access and car parking.

Of course there are ideal solutions, but only the Dutch and the Danes, it appears, have the middle class conscience and the social discipline to take them. In Holland a large, beautiful town like Haarlem can close virtually every inner street of its historic commercial centre to all except cyclists and walkers and still the shops flourish. Cheltenham could, as the garden town of England, go appropriately green. It could declare: 'We have reached a limit of commercial profitability beyond which we will not try to advance. If you do not like our policy, go and live somewhere else. If you want to shop

One small section of the great vacancy which now lies north of the High Street and west of Holy Trinity, waiting for a sane housing programme.

here, visit here, see films and plays or attend to your business in enviable green surroundings then you must walk, cycle or use our flawless, punctual, gliding public transport because it is a rule here that everyone, even our Chief Executive, leaves his car in the garage.'

Simply to write such a proposition is to realise its impossibility, though not its impracticality. It would be perfectly practical but there is no will. Some day perhaps, but in our still class-ridden society, status depends as much upon the make and use of a car as it ever did in earlier days upon a horse and carriage. We covet our travel in isolation and will ravage the entire infrastructure of a town in order to preserve it.

What makes the tedious problem of traffic relevant to this study is the way in which Cheltenham's politicians, desperate for trade and always conscious of the twin town, Gloucester's rival attractions, have sacrificed the town's architectural fabric in an effort to accommodate all comers on their own terms. The centre has been pocked with car-parks leaving whole quarters north of the High Street desolate, areas that should be alive with trade and with residents eager for that trade. In one matter, Reg Ward's survey of the Cheltenham scene was correct when it analysed the physical narrowness of the town's shopping area. Two main streets are a mean shopping base for 100,000 inhabitants. Only one short block north from the High Street up North Place or Winchcombe Street comes an ugly emptiness of parked cars beside Holy Trinity church. Another miserable vacancy lies alongside St James's Street. The council demolishes Regency housing not to invest in a new infrastructure, but to sell parking tickets.

A simple failure of projected enterprises explains these hollow areas that have been allowed, in the case of the

A car-park on luckless Albion Street.

Portland Street car-park alongside Holy Trinity, to sap away the town's natural vitality. The owners of each depressing emptiness wait hopefully for a rich developer to come along with schemes for new hotels and office blocks, projects that will produce high ground rents or rich selling prices. The Council owns both the Portland Street car-park and the old coach station site. It is the Council's duty to develop both. What Cheltenham needs to fill these ugly holes is new housing with shops on their southern fringes along St Margaret's Road. 'If people live near where they work in town, in flats and houses, or over shops, then crime and vandalism are easier to combat': sound advice from a Department of the Environment document of 1994. If Cheltenham wants to revitalise its heart streets, the way to do it is by bringing back the residents from those isolated suburbs of the outer 'doughnut' ring, not by expelling the workers from a gentrification south of Francis Close Hall as Reg Ward's 'Bid' proposes. All around this northern sector of the town in St Paul's and Fairview is a fascinating range of late classical housing, not designed crudely for 'the working class' but moving by subtle gradations of class, or more precisely of prosperity level, from lowest artisan to lower middle class. Almost all the houses are stuccoed and white. They have sun-reflecting surfaces with little indicators of rank that vary from street to street – the fanlights, the window architraves, the porches, the plaster flowers on keystones, the delicate acanthus wreaths on supporting brackets. This is the Cheltenham that tourists miss. These are the houses to which modern architects should turn, if and when they are allowed to regenerate the car-parks with people again.

The deserts between Holy Trinity and the western boundary of the old coach station could contain a large village. What it should contain if the Council became tough with developers and car pressure groups, is a sequence of four urban squares, complements to Clarence and Wellington, as varied as Portland Square in Fairview, as playfully ornate and individual as the houses of Dunalley Parade. There must be mixed use – workshops, pubs and shops. The St Paul's area and Fairview are a revelation of how many Lilliputian factories can exist organically and harmlessly in the middle of a residential area. Planners have killed whole districts of our towns by their purist formulae of the separation of work, residence and play. Here in north Cheltenham they could make their apologies. There is no need for the Council to experiment upon the streets around the Lower High Street. The new Urban Village Reg Ward is looking for could begin tomorrow on the virgin site of Holy Trinity car-park and the old coach station, with two new, mixed use streets on that vacuum off St James's Street as an additional bonus to regeneration. Planners and traffic engineers forget that people who live in towns, as opposed to suburbs, walk, because they rarely need cars.

As for the cars themselves there is a solution if the Council can control their own dreams of grandeur and of massive developers' deals. Along the Chelt, behind the fat hulks of two ill-considered office blocks, lies the St James's station site, at present a long-stay car-park, ten acres in extent. Chestergate developers have been looking at it for some time and the County Council has toyed with it as a site for new Magistrates' Courts. It is a near miracle, a car-park for 800 cars that could be extended over waste ground and doubled by an underground deck to take 2,500 cars, all within a few minutes of the town centre and all lying, by a fluke of the terrain, almost out of sight. Most towns would commit murder for such an asset. Charge a modest fee for a three-hour stay and a crippling extra for anything over that time. Service it with a bus leaving punctually every five minutes for an inexpensive circular ride around the town's shops, and any more ambitious schemes of 'park-and-ride' out at the Racecourse could be abandoned. The bus would only really be needed for the old, infirm and idle because the St James's site is so amazingly convenient, but as shopping bags are heavy it must run at frequent intervals with predictable regularity.

Anyone who supposes that Cheltenham's abject surrender to the car has been exaggerated should take a walk around old St Mary's church, left lonely and under-used by the Dean Francis followers of evangelical St Matthew's. It is as if motorised ants had been gnawing away at the entire urban fabric. Immediately west of the churchyard itself is the void of 'Britannia Parking'. Along St George's Place, next to The Vaults pub, is another car-park then, hollowed out under No.39 by a new archway, is again a little car-park, crushed into a one-time back garden, and across the graveyard of St George's Chapel, there is, predictably, another untidy puddle of parked cars. Four parking areas within a stone's throw of each other, in the very centre of a town surrounded by car-parks and consequently ravaged by incessant traffic. The only cure is replanting and rebuilding these ruined spaces and imposing, as Bristol has done so bravely, savage ramps intended not so much to 'calm' traffic as to crack the axles and smash the exhaust units of anything crossing them at more than 10 mph. Yet the Chief Executive is proposing new, fast roads into the town and new business blocks to create even more traffic: all in the name of 'employment'.

Reg Ward's Bid – the Road and the Crop Circle

The Reg Ward plan – 'Cheltenham Millennium' – was a gallant attempt by a Chief Executive, Colin Nye, to respond to a period of recession and unemployment in the town. It must be added that it was also grandiose, unsympathetic and ill-conceived, being based on one man's previous work experience of converting a dockland slum in London into a flashy, government subsidised business centre. The plan was estimated to cost £200 million but, in the usual optimistic way of such schemes, with only 'a small imput from the Borough Council's existing budgets'. The Government was to 'kick start' the project with £6,250,000, the rest coming from an eager private sector. Needless to say, the Government turned down this chance to spend six million pounds in a scheme to turn Cheltenham into the same dreary mess as Croydon. Reg, Colin Nye and their docile supporters on the Borough Council's majority group were not dismayed by this setback. Their news sheet, *The Clarion*, claimed that Reg and his team were 'revising the plans, finding different methods of funding' and still expected 'to make a start on building later this year' (1995).

So the threat still hangs over the town. Clearly there must be enormous profits to be made on the St James's site if Reg is so confident that 'new partners from the private sector', as *The Clarion* described them, are ready to invest on such a scale.

If the Ward plan is ever put into action, it will not so much rescue Cheltenham from a temporary difficulty as transform it into a different, inferior town, burdened with even more traffic and sprouting a heavy crop of second-rate office blocks in artificial stone.

When Mr Ward descended on Cheltenham from his interrupted retirement in the early 1990s, it must have seemed to local businessmen that the great days of the Spa's expansion in the 1820s were returning. As Joseph Pitt had driven Cheltenham out boldly to the north and Thomas Billings and the Jearrads had built with vision to the south, so Reg Ward would now finance and persuade a new axis of the town into existence, far out to the west, beyond the abattoir, Tesco and the old gasworks to the railway lines. Those earlier precedents may not have been entirely happy, as most of their entrepreneurs went bankrupt, but at least they had left fine things behind them.

Reg had presided from 1981 to 1988 as Chief Executive of London Docklands Development Corporation, with a light railway as its catalyst and an 800 foot tower block as its half-tenanted icon. It was Colin Nye who brought him out of retirement to kick-start, so it was hoped, the town's economy into new life.

What Reg produced was his 'Bid' – 'Cheltenham Millennium, a Single Regeneration Budget'. The 'Bid' is a fat, nine chapter handout with coloured maps. It is

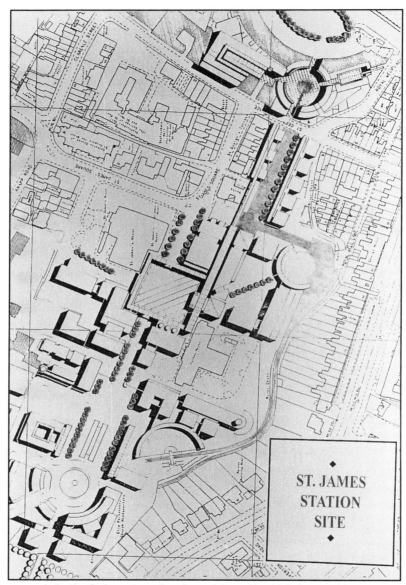

ST. JAMES
STATION
SITE

*The scale of Reg Ward's proposals for the St James's station site and the traffic which they would generate are apparent from this plan.
St James's House and Fulton House already occupy part of the area. Will new municipal offices be housed in one of the crescents?*

written in an enthusiastic developers' jargon of 'matrixes', 'synergy' and 'exponential increases'. Some paragraphs actually end, as in an early Barbara Cartland novel, with a row of dots. But it has been cleverly researched, and even though it ignores the town's official, limp, cliché-ridden *Local Plan* of 1991, it puts forward enough ingenious suggestions for financing its projects to rouse the hopes of any institutions prepared to take risks on the chance of future gain.

Imbedded in the hype and the destructive axial nonsense of the 'Bid' is the commonsense observation that a large area of vacant land out around the town's old gasworks has been linked quickly and safely to the M5 by the improved Tewkesbury Road. If further development were to take place on that unprepossessing gasworks site, it would do minimal damage to the town's image and impose few extra hardships on the town's transport system.

The Reg Ward Bid aims, however, at projects far more ambitious and potentially damaging. For its catalyst it would depend upon a major new road, and for its icon Reg has chosen an extraordinary new construction shaped like a crop circle with two outflung arms. Lured by that eastern gasworks vacancy, he has proposed a great axial thrust of development and prosperity to redress what he sees as 'an insufficient critical mass on and around the Promenade. It is too one-sided a centre to grow.' With a weakness for geometrical shapes that is Freemasonic in its obsessiveness he projects a triangle of wealth. This is to have its mystic apex in the dead centre of the municipal offices on the Promenade and its baseline on the British Rail sidings. Such a triangle would have, he urges, 'the synergy created by the inter-action between adjacent and often radically different areas'. Unfortunately none of these adjacent areas is at present linked with any of the others – Royal Crescent,

St James's long-stay car-park, abattoir or gasworks – hence the need for the road and the Crop Circle to create that 'synergy'.

The road is, hopefully, to be financed by private firms eager to gamble on a subsequent rise in land values. Leaving St George's Road at the point where that crosses the old Honeybourne line, it will sweep via four large 'circulatories' along the course of the little river Chelt, thereby negating any chance for ever of turning that luckless channel into a park feature. Through the school playing fields, which Reg aims to replace by 'all-weather playing facilities' on another site, the road will drive through the market at the abattoir, through the Texas store, Lower Mill Street, Collett Drive and the old gasworks site to curve boldly into the Tewkesbury Road right through the Co-op store, and just missing B and Q. It would not, therefore, be a cheap item, but hugely expensive.

The Crop Circle is more obscure in its function, but when he comes to listed buildings and Regency heritage Reg Ward seems to sense that the ground is beginning to quake. Still he must have his triangle, and to obtain this flow of customers and commerce, this 'synergy', eastward from the Promenade, a pedestrian route is to be created through 'the restoration of Royal Well and a strengthened context of the Municipal Buildings'. Quite how this 'context' is to be strengthened by piercing one of the greatest terraces in Europe and removing the municipal offices to another site (which he reveals is his intention on pages 26 and 27 of his Bid) is just one of the document's harebrained paradoxes. Ward should know from past failures on the Docklands project that there may not be quite such an eager rush of companies wanting to build on the St James's station site as his Bid projects; this is Cheltenham, not the Isle of Dogs, and we are in the austere 1990s. In that case it would be

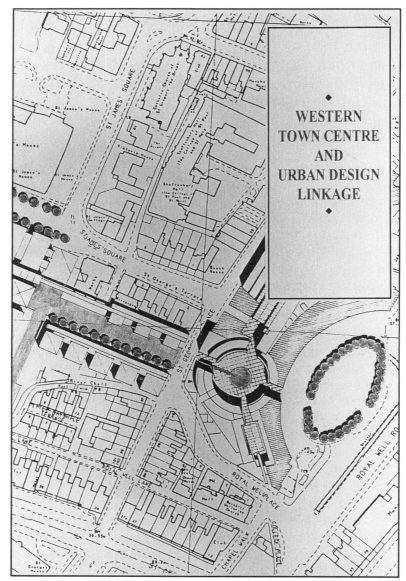

This plan from Reg Ward's 'Bid' shows the Royal Crescent pierced for the Crop Circle but not crossing St George's Place, a main traffic artery.
The historic synagogue can just be distinguished compressed between new blocks along a Reg pool.

convenient to give an impression of healthy activity on the vacant lots by building a new, inferior and quite unwanted set of municipal offices out there, with a consequent rise in the town's council tax for several years. His visionary layout for the site has a grandiose crescent overlooking a lake pumped up from the Chelt. Could this be the new municipal offices in embryo? A literal case of priming the pump for future investment.

Ward's revamped Royal Well is another wild paradox: its 'restoration' is to be achieved by removing the bus station and turning it, in 'the medium term' into a car-park, yet another to add to the town's galaxy of visual depression. The bus station will be re-sited in the narrow, one-way Albion Street in order to revive, so the Bid suggests, the commercial viability of the Beechwood Centre. The Bid aims to reduce the number of empty shops in Cheltenham by creating even more shops there around Albion Street, in the Lower High Street and, though this is left vague, in the side arms that are to flail out around the Crop Circle.

To reach the Crop Circle from this 'restored' car-park in Royal Well, the Bid's plans show a clear slice cut asymmetrically through the Royal Crescent into the adjacent amphitheatre of the Crop Circle with a central pool. To be fair to Reg Ward, his description of this circular structure is not 'the Crop Circle'. At one point he calls it 'a high quality new urban design-led linkage'; at another it is 'a superbly elevated pedestrian arcade that is carried across St George's Place and at ground level it creates distinguished spaces and uses related to the renovated buildings that exist towards St James's Square'. Developers have to learn to write in this style.

In hard reality, the 'linkage' appears to be an overhead pedestrian walkway of the type that has become a mugger's gold mine in other towns. It would destroy one of the town's few Art Nouveau buildings and there

The old Winter Gardens reborn in the Beechwood Centre off the High Street – functional in its levels, crude in its detail, the water effects and the tropical vegetation are a wholehearted delight, perfectly appropriate to the town's past.

would be room under it for itinerants and perhaps for skateboarding. Confusingly, the detailed plans in the Bid do not show it as crossing St George's Place at all.

Royal Crescent with a concrete bus-shelter and recent mural decoration.
Reg Ward's 'Bid' appears to propose piercing the Crescent behind the two trees.

But that road happens to be a section of Cheltenham's extended inner ring road which the Bid twice suggests might need revision, though it never gets down to the direction of such revision. The vagueness is tactical, as one undoubted effect of the 'revitalisation' of the St James's station site, all ten acres of it, which is the core of the Bid's proposals, would be to increase substantially the traffic pouring into the town either by this route from the Promenade and St George's Place or from St George's Road and the new road projected along the Chelt. So there would be no question of removing or even revising the ring road in the future.

Behind all its fine social aspirations, Reg Ward's Bid is an attempt to rescue Cheltenham from what is claimed to be a desperate situation by turning it into a larger, uglier town with an increased traffic problem. All the talk of creating 'the resources needed to maintain its Regency fabric' is eyewash. Where the 'Regency fabric' is not having holes bored through it to increase pedestrian flow to 'a very large multifaceted development site, the St James's site', it would be being shaken by the pounding of extra traffic drawn into the centre, exactly the traffic that would be discouraged by a wiser proposal.

That 'multifaceted development' to be extended around Jessop Avenue and the melancholy hulks of St James's House and Fulton House, stranded in their parking areas, would begin where the Crop Circle dropped its pedestrians at a ruler-straight lake of water pumped up from the Chelt. The historic synagogue would be crushed up against a new block. As for the design of the many new buildings and crescents airily sketched in to occupy the present car-park, this is the weakest section of all the developers' hype.

Richard Rogers has admitted in the 1995 Reith lectures that business firms always build as cheaply as local

The realities of any new business park – Fulton House on the old St James's station site.

authorities will allow. In this case the local authority's powers would be minimal, as the Bid proposes to rely on private money for most of the infrastructure and private money is certain to drive some very hard bargains. There would be no stucco because the upkeep is expensive. Instead there would be banal 'tasteful' facades in pre-cast concrete or reconstructed stone units. When any preliminary model was prepared, green sponge would be applied liberally to suggest a leafy setting. The subsequent reality would be car-parks and evergreen shrubs in beds of bark chippings. Indifferent to economic realities, the Bid rattles on about 'an exciting counter-point between the existing Regency and new Modern design' – hype-speak for a conflict between imaginative old historic building and cheap modern minimalism. For all his written lip-service to our 'magnificent Regency Heritage', Reg Ward reveals himself in oral briefings as disliking the contrast between Regency fronts and Regency rear elevations. Groupies for classical architecture do not rise to the head of Dockland development areas.

So the Bid proposes this 'bargain basement' prosperity sphere on the St James's site. Then to the west the new Reg-Way will divide any further developments from the Chelt which will run, like the ditch it is at present, between the road and existing housing. The school playing field would go for more office units, so would the market and the Texas store. There is no need to offer any criticism of the developments that Reg Ward proposes for the old gasworks and railway sidings. All that matters is that these should not be connected by any 'vision thing' with the town's inner street system. The Reg-Way must never be built. It would create, not solve, problems. His thinking, where traffic engineering is concerned, is ten years out of date. The same criticism could be levelled at the Borough's general policy on roads. Social problems are not solved by hurling road works at them.

An interesting feature of the Bid which has been left to the last is Reg's proposal to create, as a modish device between New Street and St Paul's Road, a new 'urban village', justified as 'a nationally significant "pilot project" alongside the Prince of Wales's Urban Villages concept'.

When the Bid's proposals are read closely this 'Urban Village' is only a polite cover for a scheme of gentrification. Here, close to the town centre, is a potentially valuable area of land between Francis Close Hall and New Street. Unfortunately it is occupied by the 'artisan' class in individual houses and a very few flats. If the workers and their small workshops can be eased out, the middle classes can be eased in with a fat increase in rents and house values. That is the reality behind the claim in the Borough's free news sheet, *The Clarion*, that 'the scheme could have resulted in over a thousand new and improved homes' and the Council's crocodile concern for 'people who are out-of-work, live in a poor environment, have poor health and exhibit many of the signs of personal deprivation'. There is an old saying, 'Beware of the Greeks when they come bearing gifts.' It might be updated to read, 'Beware of developers when they come offering to help the working classes.'

Now it is a fascinating social certainty that middle class developers automatically hate, loathe, detest and strive to destroy an area of successful working class, or as the politically correct have it, 'artisan', housing. They hate it because by offering first-time buyer homes at reasonable prices it keeps house prices and rents down. They loathe it because they could not bear to live there themselves cheek-by-jowl with neighbours 'in narrow streets that exhibit all the normal features of deprivation and sub-standard environment', so Reg writes, unprotected by front gardens from a 'common' pavement. They detest it because it works organically and efficiently with what Reg scornfully calls 'low grade, low cost, low employment uses – Builders' Yards, Storage and Car-related activities'. But these are the contemptible service industries of the kind we all turn to in everyday emergencies, where the works premises are situated only a minute's walk from the workman's breakfast table. Finally, developers seek to destroy such areas in the name of progress because there are rich pickings to be had. The Bid carefully notes, street by street, the houses that could be renovated and priced up, then notes gloatingly that if 'low grade business operations' were removed to expensive, inconvenient out-of-town sites, there would be room in the new 'urban village' for 290 new houses. The present £350,000 per acre value of the area for residential building would rocket and if the old occupants, isolated by then in a block of flats on the outskirts, ever regretted their lost privacy and their little back gardens, who would care? Bother the working classes; they don't know what's good for them. Had not Gloucestershire Health identified their old homes as 'the most socially deprived area of the Town'? But has Reg Ward heard also that working class flats, like pedestrian walkways, breed crime? Faced with the choice, would he not prefer his own house and back garden on Grove Street to a two bedroom flat two floors up on Hester's Way?

Francis Close Hall, an outlier of the Gloucestershire College of Higher Education, is used by the Bid to give an acceptable social front to this Urban Village. It will 'reach out into the whole area between Swindon Road and Lower High Street' despite the fact that the awful Northern Relief Road already separates it from them.

Reg proposes a pedestrian bridge of 'a simplistic wooden design' – his words – to span the gap 'establishing a new context for the housing, creating employment, environmental and leisure activity spaces as part of a new community base for the College'. And, of course, raising land values. But the notion of a frail, wooden bridge over a four-stream highway to link the catering department of a college to a new area of bourgeois housing is an instance of the Ward Bid's tenuous grasp of practicalities.

One entirely sensible proposal in the whole shaky edifice of the Bid is that Cheltenham's Market should leave its gloomy abattoir site and become a Portobello Road-style street market in a largely pedestrianised Lower High Street. That would do more to attract shoppers to the town than any number of synergetic matrices. Quite how a street market would co-exist with the inner ring road is not explained!

If Reg Ward's Bid nose-dives into its own contradictions and pretensions it will only join a number of such plans and proposals, launched by the over-busy in the last hundred uninspiring years. What its mere existence does imply is that the town, or at least the townspeople who contrive to get themselves elected to public office, has never come to terms with its essential decorative function. It must be a place in which to enjoy living rather than somewhere to make a fortune. One day, someone official will notice that most towns worth living in have, at some time, declined in population, but that day will not come until Reg is back in retirement. If Cheltenham continues with its present system of council officers there will be future Chief Executives, and it would be desirable that they have an interest in historic buildings and a knowledgeable enthusiasm for classical architecture as well as an interest in promoting the town.

Sinful Style –
A Twentieth Century Puritanism

There are reasons for Cheltenham's dismal record of philistine indifference over the last fifty years. Some are obvious enough: a population over-weighted with the retired and with newcomers, the cliché of the town as a social joke at the other end of the scale from Wigan, and the national insistence on full employment linked with capitalism's penchant for cutting corners. But behind all these were a set of thoughtless and destructive assumptions about style. Critics of architecture in the twentieth century have tended to be led by architects, not, as in the nineteenth century, the other way round. Architects want employment; the firms who commission them want cheap buildings, and the standardised units that can offer cheap building are readily available. Architects and critics have to work harmoniously together. New buildings provide copy for exciting newspaper and magazine articles; the more revolutionary their style and shape, the better the write-up. But what the architectural journalists have found difficult has been to move aesthetically from praising some innovative, one-off monster of glass, steel and concrete to a just assessment of another design in a traditional historicist style. Praise for the first apparently demanded scorn for the second.

There was no inevitable logic to this, but it appears that the whole dreary aesthetic doctrine of 'simple clean lines', which has prevailed in the West ever since the Bauhaus, was a conspiracy, subconscious possibly, between theoreticians, architects and patrons to excuse cheap construction. Ornament became a dirty word because it became the preserve of expensive, hyped artists rather than of cheap, waged craftsmen.

The result of these essentially economic aesthetics has been to blunt and bewilder popular taste. There was, particularly after 1945, when it became widely known that Hitler had been a neo-classicist, a general feeling in the West that 'modern' design, simple, clean and cheap, was moral design. Hence, for decades, the sheer tedium and shoddiness of most modern buildings was not discussed: a pure case of an emperor with no clothes. In retrospect it is remarkable how a number of architectural historians of real distinction and scholarship became brainwashed into acceptance of the unacceptable. The influence of Nikolaus Pevsner and John Summerson was pervasive. It was as if these eminent old men were proving their aesthetic credibility by being unshockable. In one sense they betrayed us all, for a younger generation of journalists and critics stormed along after them imposing the same opinion.

Ordinary bureaucrats who gravitated to planning offices, conservation posts and county architect's offices inevitably shared in these accepted aesthetics and played safe. To build in historic styles required an extra training that was rarely on offer. Their

Scholarly Reproduction at its best – the new end pavilion to complete one of Cheltenham's more magisterial terraces, Queen's Parade.

Kentucky Fried Georgian terraces like these tend to be mocked but usually sit admirably in Cheltenham's lesser streetscapes.

This end pavilion on a Rodney Road terrace is a successful essay in Progressive Classicism replacing an unusually bad glass and concrete block.

bewilderment is perfectly expressed in the only written guide to style that Cheltenham Borough Council, under the constraints of national legislation, offers to prospective builders in the town. Section 2 of the 1991 *Local Plan Review* starts with a fatal show of hand washing: 'Only exceptionally should they [local planning authorities] control design details if the sensitive character of the area or the particular building justifies it', an extraordinary disclaimer of responsibility in a town at least half of which is 'sensitive'. But then follow the real contradictions and vacuous cop-outs:

There will be some circumstances, such as a replacement building in a terrace, where a building of an older, contemporary style will be specifically required, but generally the Council prefers buildings which belong, honestly, without apology, to the present day.

There is no need to look any further to understand the inexorable degradation of Cheltenham's five Regency suburbs – the bungalow church of the Christian Scientists on Bayshill Road, the National Westminster's brutal extension on Suffolk Road, the complete banality of Inland Revenue House on Parabola Road. They all belong, 'honestly, without apology,' to the present day. But then the *Local Plan* changes tack to cover itself:

> The Council will otherwise prefer a good reproduction 'Regency' building to a mediocre modern building. Buildings designed in older styles will have to be of an appropriate and convincing design, entirely accurate in all details and inter-relationship of parts.

Whoever wrote that sentence clearly had no time for Post-Modernism. Indeed it was fascinating to see the storm of angry prose poured out in the quality press during the 1980s when Post-Modernism looked likely to

Park Place flats replaced a dull hotel. Their designer toyed with Post-Modernism as if nervous of spending too much money on bold detail.

consign Modernism to the dustbin. Section 2.16 of the *Local Plan* ends with a self-righteous note of political correctness: 'a permanent record of the date of construction will be required to be displayed on the main facade.' How much more satisfying it would be if the names of the architects of Inland Revenue House and the National Westminster extension were required to be carved in letters six inches high over the entrances of their buildings.

Two recent houses on Tivoli Road are hopelessly wrong in scale.

An architect's impression of the new additions to the terrace on Montpellier Spa Road. These are flats, not houses, a cautious but sympathetic design with a politically correct date on its cornice.

Does Pegasus Court on St Stephen's Road qualify as Post-Modern or Pastiche?

What Cheltenham residents and Cheltenham's planning and conservation officers need is not this crude binary split between 'honest' modern and 'accurate' older styles, but a lively awareness of the merits and suitability of the six styles currently available to architects and to design-and-build teams in the town. Then, if a prospective developer is not prepared to find a design in the style most appropriate to the site, he or she should be firmly directed to a distant borough with lower standards. Despite alarm over the 'Peace Dividend' and local unemployment, Cheltenham is not in the position of London's Docklands, where thousands of square feet of office space were going begging and any inducement or subsidy was used to lure new firms and businesses into a near-disaster area that had been grossly and often drearily over-built.

What is needed is informed debate about the six possible styles that are available for new projects. The six often overlap contentiously, but a little healthy contention in Cheltenham will educate the Council out of its current naive stylistic simplifications. The six are:

Scholarly Reproduction as in 10 Queen's Parade, 1 Lansdown Crescent, Fairview Court.
Progressive Classicism – Royscot House on the Promenade, Greville Park.
Post-Modernism – Corinth House on Bath Road, the new Library extension, Lypiatt Mews.
Pastiche - Pegasus Court, St Stephen's Road.
Modernism – can take many forms: glass and steel, concrete blocks, plastic sausage shapes, all usually un-neighbourly, often 'exciting'.
Contemporary Vernacular – Vernon Court off Sandford Park, Tom Price Close.

The first, *Scholarly Reproduction*, has its obvious and accepted place in the completion of great symmetries. It was not deployed when one of the fine villa sequences on Parabola Road suffered some damage from a German bomb in 1940. It should have been, and Parabola has been visually crippled by Elizabeth House ever since.

Tebit House on Winchcombe Street, a half-hearted exercise in Post-Modernism with a residential court to the rear.

Vernon Court, a coy gabled refuge for business activities –
Contemporary Vernacular at its most self-effacing.

Elizabeth House on Parabola Road replaced a handsome villa
bombed, but by no means destroyed, in the 1939-45 war.
It makes a drab interlude in a fine villa sequence.

College View on Douro Road picks up the spirit of Regency
classicism with immaculate detail and livlely invention.

Two highly successful examples of *Progressive Classicism* have been built recently in Cheltenham, one subtly just out of its correct context, the other perfectly at home. The first is College View on Douro Road. An enchanting circular house in the true spirit of Regency frivolity, it is very slightly too clever for its staid Victorian neighbours. The second is a mews development, a restrained but rewarding brick and

Heathfield Lodge on Central Cross Drive, Pittville fills a modest mews statement with interesting detail – an idiosyncratic 'one-off' but in exactly the right place.

Post-Modernism is a dangerous style because it depends upon wit and it is questionable whether any joke can ever be permanent. It emerged as a style in the early 1980s as a protest against tedium by a generation of architects who had been conditioned not to take the real

stucco, temple-style cottage, Heathfield Lodge, on Central Cross Drive, behind Pittville Lawn. Cheltenham's mews lanes offer so much more freedom for ingenuity of design than her main streets and this small temple has seized that liberty.

The always arguable difference between *Progressive Classicism*, *Post–Modernism* and *Pastiche* is one of commitment. In the former, the architect takes up classical details and proportions and evolves them, using them to create a twentieth century building of real classical feeling and scale, whether playful classicism as in College View, or sober domestic classicism as at Heathfield Lodge. In *Post-Modernist* buildings one or more classical motifs are applied self-consciously but boldly on an otherwise modern structure. *Pastiche* plays insipidly and delicately with classical detail, never aiming to be authentic but only to suggest a token classical air. It is common in repro work of the 1930s rather than in modern design.

The new Library building on Chester Walk, a bracing but ruthless exercise in Post-Modernism.

Post-Modernism in mild domestic register on Lypiatt Mews.

classical orders seriously. Hence, there is a certain quality of self-disparagement in that new wing to the Library on Chester Walk. It is an endless nudge in the ribs to those claiming to be visually sophisticated. Yet in that new, low, Eagle Star building on the Bath Road, the office block disguised as Regency stables, *Post-Modernism* works well.

The last style of the six, *Contemporary Vernacular*, is usually insidiously ordinary, giving the appearance of standard council housing (see Suffolk Mews) or tricked out with meaningless little gables (see Vernon Court). It can in skilled hands fit unassumingly into quiet corners, human in scale, cosy in feeling. Cheltenham's favourite handling of the style involves brown brick, which is always wrong in a Regency town of light-reflecting surfaces. Pate Court on the Northern Relief Road is a large, well-intentioned but visually depressing example of the style on a particularly public and blighted site. We have to do better than this.

A College and its Context
– The Park

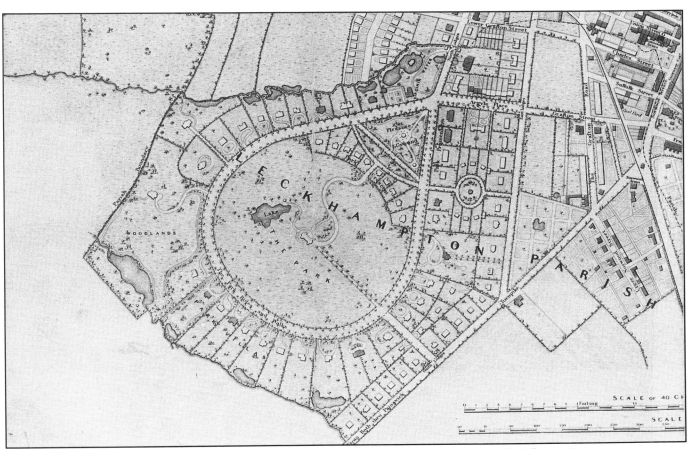

The Park loop as it should have been developed. Cornerways now stands at its apex. Park Crescent was never built; the proposed Learning Centre is to rise near its left-hand wing overlooking the lake.

Over the next few years The Park is likely to become the test case for Cheltenham's self-awareness and self-preservation. As the Ladies' College depressed a key area of the town in the past, so the Gloucestershire College of Higher Education, seeking university status, threatens that green loop of trees, lawns, lake and fine villas. Nothing is more damaging to a town's infrastructure than a confident institution, be it hospital or college, in an expansionist mood. It tends to be self-righteous and hard to block because it will claim to serve the public, not itself. Half of The Park loop is still lawns and trees. It could easily become a campus of discordant blocks put up as the money becomes available, one-off gestures by architects eager to take advantage of the flattering setting which their designs will then downgrade. A Learning Centre may offer a view from its glass walls of the lake but what of the view from the lake of the Learning Centre?

There may well be a plan afoot to demolish Fullwood, a large brown brick student hostel with spartan plumbing, and to replace it with villa-type student residences appointed luxuriously enough to attract the profitable conference trade during vacations. If these are built, and the idea is admirable, they will be neighboured by earlier villas of outstanding architectural quality like Cornerways and Longford, so their design will be a challenge.

An interesting precedent might be suggested, one that will have the architectural journalists of the national broadsheets hooting with contemptuous laughter or strident with rage, but that could give Cheltenham the chance to return to the local builders who first made the town an Elysium.

Down Merestones Road, a consortium called Taywood Homes is building an estate of five-bedroom villas in a Regency styling so convincing that it could be described as *Scholarly Reproduction* rather than *Progressive Classicism*. True to Picturesque theory, the villas are set casually on winding drives and closes with variant fenestration, Doric porches and wrought iron verandas. Being attractive, diverse and openly bourgeois, they will not please the self-appointed avant-garde but it would be a safe bet that in a hundred years time these villas of Greville Park, as the estate is called, will have become an essential stop on the Cheltenham tourist round.

If Taywood Homes can adapt basically standard units so imaginatively it should not be beyond the ingenuity of an architectural practice or a design-and-build team to devise larger, equally authentic Regency villas for student-conference occupation. They would need to be boldly differentiated from each other, like Quinlan Terry's new villas on Regent's Park in London, and they should be in stuccoed harmony with their context: the existing villas of The Park. All the vice-chancellor of the new university would need would be the courage to confront the angry apostles of discordant modernism.

Those villas are for the future; of more pressing interest is the glass and steel design which the Percy Thomas Partnership is proposing for the new Learning Centre to be constructed among the trees and green spaces of that part of The Park loop which has not yet been covered with academic bric-a-brac. It is an impressive design as might be expected from such a distinguished, experienced architectural practice. Almost everyone who sees the drawings is delighted. Three storeys high, delicately transparent, with a wide steel parasol extending above it and outwards around it on slender branching supports, it then rises even higher with a darker, hunched service area, hangar-like as though to contain a vice-chancerial helicopter. All around it, of course, veiling and flattering its fragilities, are the existing mature trees of The Park.

The new reception and administration building of the College of Higher Education on The Park affects a breezy seaside modernism, too delicate in detail to be called Brutalist, but better described as Muscular Feminist.

Cornerways – how Cheltenham was once able to design and build, exquisitely agonised Italianate.

A 1994 villa on Greville Park - a stylistic response to popular taste rather than to the architectural critics of the 'quality' press.

But is not this Learning Centre, the question has to be asked, yet another example of a brilliant one-off design being projected to take advantage of an existing area of natural and architectural excellence which it will then outface and downgrade by the sheer contrast between classical stucco and its modern steel and glass units? Would such an ambitious design have been offered for one of the college's less bourgeois sites, Hardwick off Swindon Road for instance? Will it permanently destroy a rare Regency Elysium with its large counter statement?

What is ironic in this case is that a director of the partnership that has devised this refined piece of environmental bad manners, Peterjohn Smyth, has written a challenging and convincingly argued article for the March 1995 issue of *Perspectives*, Prince Charles's architectural magazine, against just such a building as the proposed Learning Centre. Smyth attacks Sir Norman Foster's Sainsbury Art Centre of the University of East Anglia because, for all its undoubted elegance, it quite fails to suggest its function; and he appeals for architects to design buildings that clearly

The proposed Learning Centre, an example of how an artist's impression
can make a large, intrusive structure appear poetic and almost impalpable.

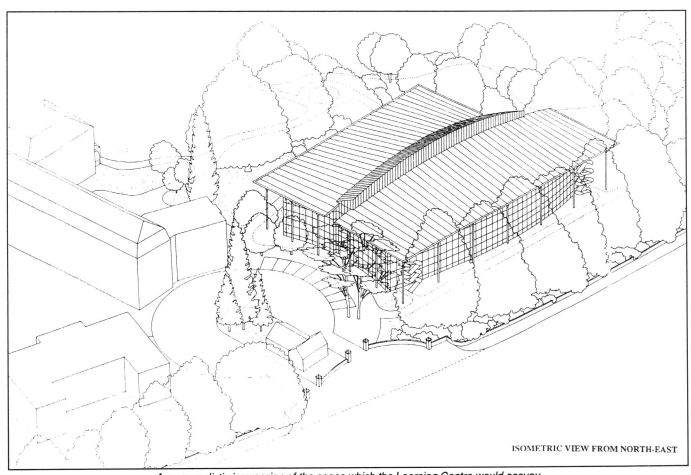

ISOMETRIC VIEW FROM NORTH-EAST

A more realistic impression of the space which the Learning Centre would occupy.

proclaim their interior role, whether church, town hall, theatre or, it must be added, Learning Centre to an institution that has deliberately chosen a gracious and historicist setting. If Peterjohn Smyth can disapprove of 'the bare concrete of London's South Bank' for its opposition to 'the cultivated Somerset House across the river', how does he view his own firm's offering of the anonymous refinement of the Learning Centre to stand against a superb sequence of classical and Italianate villas? Does this design proclaim any function or relate to its fine context?

Rather than leave these questions in the air it is helpful to consider a recent, underpraised but extraordinarily successful architectural venture in an even more demanding context: the Sainsbury Wing added by the American Post-Modernist Robert Venturi to the National Gallery in Trafalgar Square. This is unashamedly modern in its reference but equally open in its classical affiliations, related confidently to the adjoining Regency-style Gallery by giant Corinthian pilasters set about functional acreages of glass. Do we have to bring in an American every time we need to compose a modern building with a historic setting? The answer surely is 'no' and who better to devise that answer than the Percy Thomas Partnership. The architect of their proposed Learning Centre is Gerhard Hattingh who has worked in Hong Kong and Taiwan and is clearly expert in the modern international style of those places. If he were to rework his designs together with Peterjohn Smyth, lead architect for Prince Charles's Poundbury village outside Dorchester, that would be a Partnership in deed as well as in name. With the refinement retained and an appropriate classical reference added they could modify the present impression of a complex only waiting for the descent of the Thunderbird puppets.

The Next Few Years

Empty and decaying, the Methodist chapel on Henrietta Street has lost its columned portico as part of Cheltenham's undeclared war on the classical orders that once gave the town style and assurance.

No one mentioned in this book is being accused of bad faith, only of bad judgement. Internationalism is the mood of the moment: international business practices, international style. There is, therefore, a real danger that when men and women are brought into Cheltenham from outside to advise and guide the town they will, initially, be insensitive to its highly individual style and nature. In the recent past the town was seduced to accept the vandalisation of the villas. Now it seems ready to be stampeded into a huge development project of possibly inferior buildings and increased traffic problems only to solve a temporary blip in employment levels and to offer a chance of profits to those ready to gamble on the town's future.

This book has been written to caution Cheltenham residents against such a course and to remind them of the treasure they still possess. I was walking in the town recently on an early March day of brilliant blue skies after a light snowfall, with ice drops falling down from the flowering almond blossom. It is still an urban space of quite exceptional beauty and distinction. The sun reflected from stuccoed surfaces and every cornice and classical capital was radiant with light or patterned by bare branches. All we need is the confidence to pick up the twin design traditions of our past – the villa Elysium and the artisan humane – to enjoy them, to conserve them and, when necessary, to follow them.

In one respect Cheltenham has been fortunate. While Bath carefully preserved its major monuments and demolished most of its graceful, useful, artisan housing of the eighteenth century, Cheltenham had been prodigal with its great villa inheritance but kept most of its four fascinating Regency artisan quarters with their winding white ways, half-lost squares, decorative class signifiers and unexpected side alleys. These above all must be protected. Tom Price Close, with its

The architect of Fairview Court observed the scale and classical detail of that artisan estate and responded to it with perfect good manners.

characterless brown brick units, was an ominous sign of planning indifference or planning illiteracy. Fairview Court on Fairview Road was the hopeful sign: proof that modern architects still have the grace to learn from the past and work in context. Brown brick, raw and alien, but curiously attractive to Cheltenham's builders, is the enemy.

Pate Court exemplifies Cheltenham planners' love affair with brown bricks and Contemporary Vernacular.

As for car control, cars could be controlled in Cheltenham. Any further work on the pernicious Northern Relief Road should be stopped forthwith. All finance and agitation should be directed to an outer southern ring road. Most of the gaping car-parks that disfigure the town should be built on, and built on with houses, not flats, in the local idiom. The St James's station site should be removed from the temptation of developers and made the centre for Cheltenham's control of traffic. Ramps should be scattered everywhere to make drivers alert, unhappy and interested in public transport. Where drivers are concerned, gentle words of persuasion get nowhere.

There are several smaller, positive measures that could be taken to restore the town to what it once was – a triumph of the Picturesque. One quick and easy improvement would be the planting of Lombardy Poplars, not my favourite tree but a Cheltenham idiom and quick growing, to screen the rear of the Town Hall, Ellenborough House's face to the car-park and the worst

Visual squalor and parked cars in the middle of Montpellier Gardens, one of the town's two most strategic green spaces. A leisure centre is threatened.

eyesores – the Post Office building and the Texas store on the Northern Relief Road. In the same planting mood, the Broad Walk should be generously recreated on the south side of Imperial Gardens and the St James's site's new expanded car-park should be surrounded with holm oaks.

Minor structural recreations should include the ten columned Doric porte cochère on Lansdown Station and the two lost porticoes from St George's Terrace. Then to get the street market off to a brisk start, we should rebuild, preferably across the Lower High Street where it leaves St George's Square, Jenkins's Hindu Market Screen of 1823. A bold visual gesture like that would do more to raise the town's spirits than any number of business parks. It is also the kind of solid, practical gesture a rich philanthropist could be persuaded to make.

It should not need to be said, but in Cheltenham nothing can be taken for granted, so let it be laid down that by 2000 AD Montpellier Gardens should be cleared of tarmac and of the tatty Gym Centre. A restored Chinese pavilion there, as the centrepiece of a small café, would make a happy salute to the Montpellier dome across the road. Then we could have architects queuing up to devise lively classical shelters, again with a small café, to replace those painful concrete shelters in Royal Well, which must remain as a bus and coach station, convenient and central; it should never be turned into yet another car-park.

A demolition list sounds drastic but Cheltenham needs one. First would have to come the Eagle Star tower, though no doubt a gang of aesthetic deviants would rally to preserve it as a monument to Harold Wilson. Then, in this order – the block with Sainsbury and Tesco on the High Street; the Magistrates' Court; the Quadrangle on the Promenade; the Whitbread Tower;

The crass hulk of the Whitbread tower.

Ellenborough House in that dead heart which widened roads and thoughtless, talentless new buildings have created around Cheltenham Town Hall.

the block between Oriel Lodge and the Bath Road; W. H. Smith on High Street; the National Westminster additions on Suffolk Road and the Linotype Hell building – all should go.

This list is not controversial, but one last suggestion might be. Does Cheltenham really value or love its Town Hall? It has an indigestible shape and wrecks Imperial Gardens. Its acoustics are sub-standard. Across the road is a particularly offensive car-park that lays open the shamefully dull block of Ellenborough House. Could we, to celebrate the new century, build a new Town and Concert Hall on this long-stay car-park mercifully hiding Ellenborough House from the public? To keep everyone happy, the new hall could be a delicate modernist confection of glass and steel at the rear with a full-blooded Regency front of fluted Corinthian pilasters in Progressive Classicist excess. Or would it be Post-Modernism? The debate would never end, and that would be the Town Hall's best testimonial – to be a stylistic talking point for an informed, concerned and visually sophisticated electorate.

The crude link between these Bayshill villas shows most emphatically the twentieth century's aesthetic betrayal of Cheltenham's Regency classicism.

The crude link between these Bayshill villas shows most emphatically the twentieth century's aesthetic betrayal of Cheltenham's Regency classicism.